C000002003

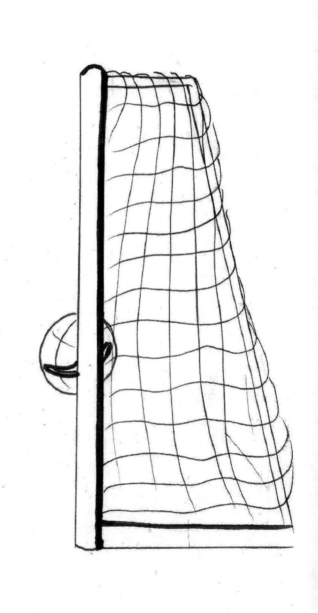

100 FACTS

Arsenal

First published in Great Britain in 2016
by Wymer Publishing
www.wymerpublishing.co.uk
Wymer Publishing is a trading name of Wymer (UK) Ltd

First edition. Copyright © 2016 Steve Horton / Wymer Publishing.

ISBN 978-1-908724-09-0

Edited by Jerry Bloom.

The Author hereby asserts his rights to be identified
as the author of this work in accordance with sections
77 to 78 of the Copyright, Designs & Patents Act 1988.

All rights reserved. No part of this publication may be
reproduced or transmitted in any form or by any means,
electronic or mechanical, including photocopying, or any
information storage and retrieval system, without written
permission from the publisher.

This publication is sold subject to the condition that it shall not,
by way of trade or otherwise, be lent, re-sold, hired out or
otherwise circulated without the publishers prior consent in any
form of binding or cover other than that in which it is published
and without a similar condition including this condition
being imposed on the subsequent purchaser.

Typeset by Andy Francis.
Printed and bound by CMP, Poole, Dorset

A catalogue record for this book is available from the British Library.

Cover design by Wymer.
Sketches by Becky Welton. © 2014.

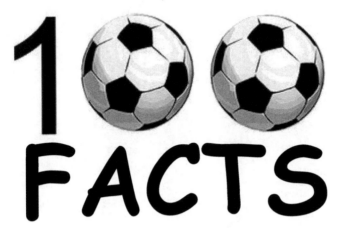

100 FACTS

Arsenal

Steve Horton

WYMER
PUBLISHING
Bedford, England

1886
THE NOMADIC
ROYAL ARSENAL FC

The football club that we now know as Arsenal was founded in 1886 by workers in the Dial Square workshop. This was part of the Royal Arsenal armaments factory in Woolwich, south of the River Thames and then situated in the county of Kent.

The workers initially called themselves Dial Square and their first match was played on 11th December on an open field at the Isle of Dogs. They beat Eastern Wanderers 6-0 and a few weeks later the name was changed to Royal Arsenal.

For the first two years the club had a nomadic existence, playing home games at Plumstead Common and the Sportsman Ground in Plumstead before settling on the Manor Ground in 1888. They were there for two years before opting to move in 1890 to the Invicta Ground where the facilities were better.

Royal Arsenal mainly played friendlies in this period but their reputation grew and in 1888-89 they got to the semi-finals of the London Senior Cup. They lost 2-0 to Clapton but this was no disgrace, as they would be the first British team to play a match in continental Europe the following year.

1889
FA CUP
DEBUT

FACT **2**

In the 1889-90 season Royal Arsenal entered the FA Cup for the first time but after a good opening win they were well beaten in the next round.

Royal Arsenal entered the competition in the third qualifying round and were drawn at home to Essex based side Crusaders. The score was 2-2 at full time but in those days extra time was played before a replay was required and they went on to win 5-2.

In the fourth qualifying round Royal Arsenal were drawn at home to Swifts, a side from Slough in Berkshire. They had a fine reputation having reached the semi-finals of the competition on three occasions.

Despite wretched weather the game attracted a huge crowd of 5,000. Sadly for Royal Arsenal they were no match for Swifts, who led 3-1 at half time. Things didn't get better in the second half as Swifts continued to dominate and the game finished 5-1.

The following season Royal Arsenal entered the competition at the first round stage and lost 2-1 at home to Derby County. This was a very respectable result as they were members of the Football League. The club did not enjoy a long cup run until 1906, when they reached the semi-finals.

1890
DOUBLE CUP
SUCCESS

Royal Arsenal tasted glory for the first time in the 1889-90 season when they won two local cup competitions, the London Charity Cup and Kent Senior Cup.

In the London Charity Cup, contested by eight teams, Royal Arsenal beat Great Marlow 4-1 at home in the first round. The semi-final gave them another home tie, this time against the 2nd Scots Guards, who were beaten 3-0. The final took place on 5th March 1890 at Leyton in front of 10,000 fans. They saw Royal Arsenal win 3-1 against Old Westminsters, a team of ex-public schoolboys.

In the Kent Senior Cup, which was being contested for the first time, Royal Arsenal beat Dartford Working Men's Club 7-1 at home in the first round. They then won 9-1 at Lewisham before hitting double figures against Ordnance Store Corps, thrashing the army side 13-1.

For the quarter-final away to Gravesend, several hundred fans travelled on a special charter train. Their journey was worthwhile as Royal Arsenal won 4-1. Folkestone were then beaten 2-1 in the semi-final at the neutral venue of Chatham. The final took place at Chatham on 22nd March 1890 and Thanet were beaten 3-0, a result which was described in the press as very popular with the majority of fans there.

1893
WOOLWICH ARSENAL
IN THE FOOTBALL LEAGUE

In the same year that Royal Arsenal changed its name the club was invited to join the Football League.

Crowds for home games had risen to 15,000 since the club had turned professional in 1891, an unusual step by a southern side. Opposition to this from other clubs in the area led to the London County Football Association banning Royal Arsenal from local cup competitions, meaning they could only compete in the FA Cup and play friendlies.

In May 1893 the club became a limited company, selling shares to enable the purchase and expansion of the Manor Ground. A return there was preferable to staying at the Invicta Ground where there was a cycle track around the pitch.

The name had to be changed to Woolwich Arsenal as privately owned companies can not have the word 'Royal' in their name. The newly named club then applied to join the Football League and on 1st June were elected to the 2nd Division along with Liverpool.

Woolwich Arsenal were London's first league club and on 2nd September they opened the 1893-94 season against Newcastle United at home before a crowd of 10,000. Walter Shaw scored the club's first ever league goal after just six minutes and the game ended 2-2.

1894
SAM HOLLIS,
THE FIRST MANAGER

There has been lots of debate over who Arsenal's first manager was. Some sources say it was Thomas Mitchell, appointed in 1897, but the club's official website credits Sam Hollis, saying he was given the role in 1894.

Before Hollis was appointed as trainer, team affairs were overseen by a committee and club members. In becoming trainer, Hollis became the first individual to have control over team selection and tactics. Hollis's appointment was an unusual one as he had little football experience, having been a former pub landlord in Nottingham.

Hollis was manager of Arsenal for three seasons, during which they finished eighth, seventh and tenth. There were no significant FA Cup runs and the club didn't win any of the local competitions. At the club's Annual General Meeting one year, it was reported that a director attended training and saw some players playing cards.

In 1897 Hollis was lured away from Woolwich by Bristol City, who were in the Southern League at the time. In 1901 he took them into the Football League but left in 1905 to run a hotel. He returned there in 1911 for two seasons and later managed Newport County.

1896
CAESAR JENKYNS,
THE FIRST INTERNATIONAL

The first Woolwich Arsenal player to represent his country was Caesar Jenkyns, who was selected to play for Wales in 1896.

Jenkyns was born in Builth Wells in 1866 but grew up in Birmingham and joined Small Heath (who later became Birmingham City) in 1888. He was a hard defender who was sent off four times, in days when rough play was part of the game and it was rare to be ordered off the field.

In 1895 he was sacked by Small Heath after trying to assault two spectators at Derby, but Woolwich Arsenal were happy to take him on and immediately installed him as captain.

As a former 1st Division player, he made quite an impact and scored six goals in 27 games. For someone so tall and well built, he was still very quick on the ball.

His performances led to him being selected in the Wales team to play against Scotland in Dundee on 21st March 1896. The *Dundee Courier* described him as being 'on a gigantic scale' and said he was the best Wales' player in a game they lost 4-0.

1895-96 turned out to be Jenkyns's only season with Woolwich Arsenal and that summer he moved to Newton Heath (later Manchester United). After retiring from football he became a policeman.

1899
HARRY BRADSHAW
ARRIVES

The first successful manager in the history of Arsenal was Harry Bradshaw, who was appointed in 1899 and led them to the 1st Division.

After Sam Hollis left, Thomas Brown Mitchell and William Elcoat each had a season in charge. Harry Bradshaw then arrived from Burnley, having led the Lancashire side to promotion and then third place in the 1st Division. It is unclear why Bradshaw chose to take over at Woolwich Arsenal, who were in financial trouble at the time.

Bradshaw liked to play a short passing game, favoured by the Scottish sides. He helped to stabilise the finances and on the pitch performances and attendances got better as the club gradually improved their position in the league table.

After finishing eighth, seventh, fourth and third Woolwich Arsenal finally achieved promotion in 1903-04 when they finished second.

During his time with the club Bradshaw's two sons were on the books but he showed them no favouritism; Joe didn't play at all and William made just four appearances in the 1903-04 season.

After achieving promotion Bradshaw mysteriously left for Fulham, who were in the Southern League. However he still goes down in history as the man who took the club into the top flight for the first time.

1900
A LEAGUE RECORD
12-0 WIN

Arsenal's biggest league victory came on 12th March 1900 when Loughborough Town were thrashed 12-0 at the Manor Ground in a 2nd Division fixture.

Back in 1896-97, Woolwich Arsenal had lost 8-0 against the Leicestershire side, a result which remains the club's biggest ever defeat. Four seasons on however, Loughborough were in financial trouble at the bottom of the league.

The visitors had won just once in 24 games and were so poor they could only afford four professional players. They even had their travel expenses paid for by the Woolwich Arsenal committee.

In glorious sunshine the first half was totally one sided with Woolwich Arsenal leading 4-0 at the break. Ernest Cottrell got two goals with the others coming from Sandy Main and Ralph Gaudie.

After the break the home side ran riot. Gaudie got two to complete his hat-trick and James Tennant and John Dick also scored two. Main added another and the rout was completed with a goal from John Anderson.

The result equalled a 12-0 win over non-league Ashford United in the FA Cup in 1893-94. The Gunners have never played Loughborough since, as they finished bottom of the league and went out of existence at the end of the season.

1904
PROMOTION

After several years of trying Woolwich Arsenal finally made it to the 1st Division when they were promoted in 1903-04.

They began the season in brilliant fashion, winning their first five games without conceding a goal and scoring 21. The club were never out of the top two before Christmas, alternating the leadership of with Preston North End.

Two successive defeats in January saw Woolwich Arsenal slip to third. They then set out on a run of five straight wins, the last of which was over nearest challengers Bristol City and opened up a five point gap.

In the final weeks of the season Preston slipped up and Manchester United went on a good run, meaning there was a thrilling three way battle for the two promotion places. In their penultimate game Woolwich Arsenal won 3-0 at Bradford, meaning just a point at home to Port Vale would be enough.

On 25th April 1904 a 0-0 draw was enough to take the club into the top flight for the first time, with Preston joining them. Woolwich Arsenal lost just six of their 34 games and were unbeaten at home. The leading scorer was Tommy Shanks with 25 goals.

1906
ARSENAL'S FIRST
ENGLAND INTERNATIONAL

The first Woolwich Arsenal player to appear for England was goalkeeper Jimmy Ashcroft, who was called up for the British Championships in 1906.

Originally from Liverpool, Ashcroft was signed by Harry Bradshaw in 1900 from Southern League side Gravesend. He was immediately installed as first choice keeper and was an ever present in 1900-01 and 1901-02. In the second of those seasons he kept six clean sheets in a row, a club record that was only matched in 1998 by Alex Manninger.

In the promotion season of 1903-04 Ashcroft kept twenty clean sheets in 34 games and he helped Woolwich Arsenal to the FA Cup semi-finals in 1906 and 1907.

Ashcroft's first England appearance was on 17th February 1906, when he kept a clean sheet in a 5-0 win over Ireland in Belfast. He did the same on 19th March when Wales were beaten 1-0 at Cardiff Arms Park. In the third match though England lost 2-1 against Scotland at Hampden Park meaning the championship was shared between those two nations.

In 1908, after 273 league appearances for Arsenal, Ashcroft was sold to Blackburn Rovers, where he won the league in 1912. He later played Tranmere before his career was brought to an end by the First World War.

1910
PROPOSED
FULHAM MERGER

With Woolwich Arsenal in financial trouble in 1910 the club looked set to merge with Fulham but the move was blocked by the Football League.

The club entered voluntary liquidation in 1910 and was then taken over by Sir Henry Norris, a property developer. He became club chairman whilst retaining a place on 2nd Division Fulham's board, leading to him proposing a merger. Norris hoped to create a London superclub which would play home games at Craven Cottage.

The Football League intervened and refused to sanction such a move, which would effectively have led to Fulham buying a 1st Division place and Woolwich Arsenal ceasing to exist.

Norris then proposed to concentrate solely on his new interest but made it clear he would move the club if the people of Woolwich did not support them.

Within three years Norris had carried out his threat to relocate the club, laying the foundations for future success.

However, he would not be in control when Arsenal dominated English football in the 1930s. This was because he was banned by the Football Association in 1929 for financial irregularities.

1913
RELEGATION AND
HIGHBURY MOVE

Sir Henry Norris carried out his threat to move Woolwich Arsenal north of the River Thames in 1913 but the club started out in their new home in the 2nd Division.

Finances at the club remained poor and Norris saw a move as the only way of securing the club's survival.

After rejecting Battersea and Harringay, Norris settled on some college playing fields in Highbury and signed deeds in early 1913. Leading stadium architect Archibald Leitch was then employed to design the stadium.

Back in Woolwich however things did not go well for the club on the pitch. A dreadful run of ten defeats in eleven games meant they were bottom of the table at Christmas and they stayed there.

The inevitable relegation was confirmed in the third from last game of the season on 12th April when Derby won 2-1 at the Manor Ground. Woolwich Arsenal finished the season with just eighteen points, scoring only 26 goals.

It meant that the first league game at Highbury on 6th September 1913 was a 2nd Division encounter with Leicester Fosse, the home side winning 2-1.

1914
'THE ARSENAL'

Despite moving to Highbury in 1913, it was not until the following summer that the Woolwich was dropped from the team's name.

Throughout the 1913-14 season when they narrowly missed out on promotion, the club retained the name of Woolwich Arsenal. All home match programmes carried this name on the cover and that was how fixtures were listed in the newspapers.

As the season went on though, some newspapers would begin news stories with 'Woolwich Arsenal' and then refer to them as 'The Arsenal'. During the close season of 1914 the company name was re-listed as 'The Arsenal Football and Athletic Club Ltd'.

Programme covers from 1914-15 have 'The Arsenal' on the cover but in 1919 the name was changed again, this time simply to 'Arsenal Football Club Limited'.

It is often believed that Herbert Chapman changed the name to Arsenal in the late 1920s but this was not the case. Programmes from 1919 onwards reflected this as they had just 'Arsenal' on the cover.

However even today media and fans often refer to the club as 'The Arsenal'. This has perhaps been most commonly displayed by the chant 'One-nil to The Arsenal'.

1919
A CONTROVERSIAL
PROMOTION

14

After competitive football was suspended for four years due to the First World War, Arsenal had a stroke of good luck in 1919 when they were promoted despite only finishing fifth in 1915.

After being relegated in 1912-13 Arsenal missed out on promotion on goal average the following season. They were further away in 1914-15 when they finished fifth, seven points behind second place Preston.

When the Football League resumed in 1919, it was decided to expand the 1st Division to 22 clubs. It was expected that the two teams who finished in the bottom two places in 1914-15 would be reprieved from relegation but that wasn't to be the case.

It was decided that nineteenth place Chelsea should retain their place but not Tottenham, who had finished bottom in 1915. Instead they were told they had to stand for election against the sides who had finished between third and eighth in the 2nd Division that year.

Arsenal chairman Sir Henry Norris argued that Arsenal deserved to be in the 1st Division due to their long league history. This was backed in a speech by Football League president John McKenna and Arsenal comfortably won the vote. They have not been relegated since and many Spurs fans point to this as the time the rivalry between the two clubs began.

1922
THE CREST

FACT **15**

After several years of using a crest based on the of Woolwich coat of arms, Arsenal finally adopted a single cannon in 1922. For the first two years there was no club crest at all then in 1888 a crest was unveiled that contained three vertical cannons, just like that of the Borough of Woolwich. This reflected the armaments factories and military hospitals in the area.

Even after moving to North London in 1913 and the dropping of Woolwich from the club name the following year the original crest remained. However when organised football began again in 1919, Arsenal memorabilia contained no sign of any crest at all.

For the 1922-23 season, the first matchday programme contained a crest consisting of a single cannon looking eastwards. Three years later this was changed to a west pointing one with the words 'The Gunners' underneath.

The crest changed again in 1949, when the cannon was placed inside a shield with the words 'Victoria Concordia Crescit' underneath. These words are Latin and translate as 'Victory grows out of harmony'.

Apart from some slight colouring changes this crest remained the same for over fifty years. In 2002 a new modern design was unveiled with the cannon facing eastward, with the only wording being 'Arsenal'.

16

1925
HERBERT CHAPMAN
ARRIVES

In 1925 Sir Henry Norris pulled off a major coup when he attracted title winning manager Herbert Chapman to Arsenal.

Leslie Knighton had been in charge since 1919 but in six seasons Arsenal failed to finish above mid table. After sacking Knighton, Norris only wanted a manager of the highest calibre and offered Chapman £2,000 a year. This was double his salary at Huddersfield where he had won the title two years running.

Chapman knew that Arsenal had great potential as they attracted bigger crowds than at Huddersfield. He made an immediate impact by signing England international Charlie Buchan, Sunderland's leading scorer.

In Chapman's first season in charge Arsenal finished second, five points behind Huddersfield. He was way ahead of his time, advocating counter attacking football, better training techniques and suggested that football broaden its horizons by having European competitions.

He set out a five year plan for success in 1925 and this was timed perfectly, as Arsenal won the FA Cup in 1930. Chapman also won two league titles with the club but died of pneumonia at the early age of 55 in January 1934. However the foundations had been laid for future success and there is a statue of him at the Emirates Stadium.

FACT 17
JOCK RUTHERFORD,
ARSENAL'S OLDEST PLAYER

The oldest player to appear for Arsenal was winger Jock Rutherford, who was 41 years and 159 days old when he played his final game for the club on 20th March 1926.

Rutherford first joined the club in 1913 from Newcastle, for whom he had played 290 times in the league. He scored twice on his Arsenal debut, when Nottingham Forest were beaten 3-2 in a 2nd Division fixture.

Despite being 35 years old when competitive football resumed after the First World War, Rutherford continued to be a regular for four seasons. Towards the end of 1922-23 he left to become player manager at struggling Stoke City, but he was unable to save them from relegation.

Rutherford returned to Arsenal in extraordinary circumstances after a retirement party held for him by his former teammates led to him resuming old friendships. He resigned from Stoke and over the next three seasons he played 45 league games, scoring four goals.

His last game was against Manchester City on 20th March 1926 and at the end of the season he left Arsenal for good and joined Clapton Orient. He was there one season and in later life went on to run an off licence.

1927
HIGHBURY STAGES
FIRST RADIO BROADCAST

On 22nd January Arsenal's home fixture with Sheffield United became the first football match in the world to be broadcast live on the radio, being one of the revolutionary ideas of manager Herbert Chapman.

The British Broadcasting Corporation (BBC) had been given a royal charter that month which allowed it to broadcast major sporting events. This was the first football match they covered but not the first sport of any kind, as the week before they had broadcast rugby union from Twickenham.

The front cover of the Radio Times divided the pitch into a grid of eight sections to assist the listeners. During the game, one of the two commentators sat in a wooden hut and would shout out the grid number where the ball was while the other described the action.

Arsenal captain Charlie Buchan scored the first goal to be broadcast on the radio. It was described by commentator Henry Wakelam, a former rugby player who had practiced his commentary technique by watching schoolboy games.

The match went on to finish 1-1 and The Times praised Wakelam's 'vivid and impressive descriptions of play'.

1927
ARSENAL'S FIRST
FA CUP FINAL

Arsenal reached the final of the FA Cup for the first time in 1927 but there was disappointment as they were beaten by Cardiff City.

The route to the final almost ended in the 4th round when Arsenal needed a late equaliser to avoid a shock exit at Port Vale. They won the replay and then beat Liverpool and Wolverhampton Wanderers at home to set up a semi-final with Southampton, who were beaten 2-1 at Stamford Bridge.

The press billed the final as England v Wales but Herbert Chapman did not make any special preparations, keeping things normal by training at Highbury.

Arsenal dominated the first half but couldn't turn their possession into goals. They began the second period well, but seemed to lose their momentum after the game was stopped due to an injury to Arsenal midfielder Jack Butler.

With sixteen minutes left Cardiff forward Hughie Ferguson hit a fairly tame shot which keeper Dan Lewis picked up only to let the ball slip through his hands into the net. Lewis, ironically a Welsh international, later blamed his mistake on his jersey being greasy.

There was no way back for Arsenal on this occasion but they have had plenty of success in the FA Cup since.

1928
NUMBERED SHIRTS

The first instance of a full team wearing numbered shirts in a football match came on 25th August 1928, when Arsenal played away at Sheffield Wednesday.

Herbert Chapman was behind the idea as he felt it would help players recognise each other. The players were numbered one to eleven according to their position, starting with the goalkeeper at number one.

On the same day as Arsenal were wearing numbers at Hillsborough, Chelsea did so in their game at Stamford Bridge. However they only gave numbers to their outfield players.

The newspapers seemed to like the idea, with the Daily Mirror commenting that 'I fancy the scheme has come to stay. All that was required was a lead and London has supplied it'. The Yorkshire Post was impressed too, saying 'the innovation was much appreciated'.

Despite the idea behind it the numbers did not do Arsenal any good on the pitch as they lost 3-2. The football authorities weren't impressed either and banned their use. Arsenal used numbers in a friendly against FC Vienna in 1933 but it was not until 1939 that they were allowed in all Football League and FA Cup games.

1929
TOM PARKER'S
APPEARANCE RECORD

In 1929-30 Arsenal captain Tom Parker made his 172nd consecutive appearance for the club, a record that is unlikely to be broken.

Formerly with 2nd Division Southampton, Parker joined Arsenal in the Spring of 1926. He made his debut on 3rd April that year against Blackburn, helping his new side to a 4-2 win.

Playing as a right back Parker did nothing special but he could always be realised on to put in a sound performance. In 1926-27 he was appointed team captain, skippering the club to their first FA Cup final.

On 26th December 1929 he played his 172nd consecutive match for the club, when Portsmouth won 2-1 at Highbury. He was then unavailable to play in the next game at Leeds two days later. Later that season he lifted the FA Cup and the following season he led Arsenal to their first Football League Championship.

At the start of 1932-33 Parker, then 35 years old, was replaced at right back by George Male. After making just one appearance all season, he left in March 1933 to become manager at Norwich City. He had played 294 matches for Arsenal, scoring seventeen goals which were mostly penalties.

In today's game of squad rotation it is hard to see Parker's record ever being broken.

1930
LEICESTER CITY 6
ARSENAL 6

The only top flight English football match to finish in a 6-6 draw involved Arsenal on 21st April 1930.

The match at Filbert Street was played on Easter Monday, five days before the FA Cup final. Herbert Chapman made a number of changes to his regular line-up, including bringing reserve striker David Halliday into the side.

In front of 25,000 fans Halliday gave Arsenal an early lead but Leicester hit back and led 3-1 at half time. Early in the second half Cliff Bastin got one back for Arsenal and then Halliday struck two in quick succession to put them 4-3 up. The three Arsenal goals had come within just ten minutes of each other.

Halliday put Arsenal further ahead only for Ernie Hine to pull one back for Leicester. Bastin made it 6-4 but Len Barry and Arthur Chandler scored for Leicester to complete a remarkable game. Despite his scoring spree, it was not enough for Halliday to be included in the cup final line-up.

The match remains the only 6-6 draw in the history of English football's top flight. Charlton and Middlesbrough drew by the same scoreline in 1960 but this was in the 2nd Division.

1930
WINNERS OF THE ZEPPELIN
FA CUP FINAL

Arsenal finally won their first major trophy in 1929-30 when they beat Huddersfield in the FA Cup final, where a German Zeppelin was a surprise visitor.

The Gunners beat Chelsea, Birmingham, Middlesbrough, West Ham and Hull to reach the final, to be contested against Herbert Chapman's former club Huddersfield. In honour of this both teams came out side by side, the first time this had happened in an FA Cup final.

In front of the watching King George V, Alex James gave Arsenal the lead in the sixteenth minute but they could not add to this before half time. Early in the second half the Graf Zeppelin, the world's largest airship, hovered overhead. At 776 feet in length, it was twice as long as the pitch and later in the day it paid a low flying visit to Buckingham Palace.

Huddersfield dominated the second half but Arsenal's defence held firm. Then with seven minutes left Jack Lambert latched on to a long clearance from James, beat two defenders and then fired the ball past the keeper to make it 2-0.

When he arrived at Highbury Chapman said it would take five years to build a winning team and he was right. This FA Cup triumph paved the way for the club to dominate the 1930s.

1931
127 GOALS WINS
THE LEAGUE

Arsenal followed up their FA Cup win by securing their first league title in 1930-31, scoring an astonishing 127 goals in 42 games.

Herbert Chapman's side won their first five league games and lost just twice before Christmas. The first three away games were all won 4-1 and other big scorelines included a 5-1 win at Chelsea and 7-1 home victory over Blackpool.

An early FA Cup exit on 24th January left Arsenal with the job of concentrating on the league and their only other loss was a 5-1 thrashing at Aston Villa. This blip aside, Arsenal routinely turned the opposition over. They hammered Grimsby 9-1 at home and a year after hitting six in a 6-6 draw at Leicester, went one better and won 7-2.

Defences were no match for the front three of Cliff Bastin, David Jack and Jack Lambert. Bastin was still in his teens but struck 28 goals in 42 games, while Lambert hit an incredible 38 from 34.

The title was secured with two games to spare when Liverpool were beaten 3-1 in front of 39,000 fans at Highbury. It was apt that Bastin, Jack and Lambert got a goal each. When the season finished they were seven points ahead of nearest challengers Aston Villa.

1932
ARSENAL
TUBE STATION

November 1932 saw the nearest tube station to Highbury have its name changed from Gillespie Road to Arsenal Highbury Hill.

The Piccadilly Line station first opened in 1906, seven years before Arsenal moved to the area. However as the club's profile grew, Herbert Chapman was concerned that visitors looking for the stadium could see no indication on underground maps of where they were situated.

On 28th October 1932 a journalist wrote in the *Islington Gazette*, "When you want to watch Arsenal play after this week, you will walk into any underground station and book a ticket for Arsenal. You will walk straight out of the station right up to the ground entrance. A fairly large section of the Arsenal crowd are from a distance and many who do not know London are at a loss to know where to book for the Gunners' ground. Months ago Mr Chapman and I discussed the subject".

The Highbury Hill part of the name was dropped in 1960 and although the club now play at the Emirates Stadium, Arsenal is still a popular tube destination for fans heading there. Links with the past remain as there is still tiling from the old days displaying the name Gillespie Road.

1933
A SECOND
LEAGUE TITLE

Arsenal won the Football League Championship for the second time in 1932-33 as they made up for the disappointment of the previous season.

In 1931-32 Arsenal finished second in the 1st Division and also reached the final of the FA Cup, where they were unfortunate to lose 2-1 to Newcastle United. Arsenal had been leading 1-0 but replays showed that Newcastle's equaliser came from a cross made after the ball had clearly gone out of play.

When the new season opened Arsenal picked themselves up from their double dose of misfortune and lost just one of their opening fourteen games. The goals were again flowing with Leicester being beaten 8-2 at Highbury and Wolverhampton thrashed 7-1 at their own ground.

There was a blip after Christmas when two successive league defeats were followed by a 2-0 loss to Walsall in the FA Cup, one of the greatest shocks in the competition's history. However the Gunners bounced back and went six games unbeaten, the highlight being an 8-0 home win over Blackburn.

The title was secured on 22nd April with two games remaining, when Chelsea were beaten 3-1 at Stamford Bridge. Arsenal finished the season four points clear of Aston Villa having scored 118 goals.

1933
WHITE SLEEVES

The white sleeves that Arsenal are famous for were worn for the first time on 4th March 1933.

It was Herbert Chapman's idea to change the kit, but there are two theories as to why he did so. One is that he saw a fan wearing a red sleeveless jumper over a white shirt, the other is that Chelsea were considering the idea and he wanted to try it out before they did.

It was believed by Chapman that the players would be able to find each other more easily with this style of shirt, and he also changed the socks to red and white hoops.

The first time Arsenal appeared in the colours they actually wore white shirts with a red pullover. Chapman telephoned Hollins & Co in Nottingham to place an order at 2:30pm on 3rd March and they were dispatched that evening, arriving in time to be worn against Liverpool.

Arsenal did actually lose the game 1-0 and failed to win any of their next three games. However the colours were not ditched and they went on to win the title.

It is unthinkable that Arsenal would ever play in anything else, although to mark the last season at Highbury they did wear a strip similar to that worn in the first season there in 1913.

1934
GEORGE ALLISON
TAKES CHARGE

Arsenal were struck by tragedy on 6th January 1934 when Herbert Chapman died of pneumonia just four days after returning from a scouting mission in Yorkshire.

Reserve manager Joe Shaw took over as caretaker manager for the rest of the season and guided the club to their third league title. However in the summer he went back to his original position and the club's managing director George Allison took over.

Allison had never played professional football and was a journalist by trade, moving to London from Darlington in 1906. He became Woolwich Arsenal's programme editor and followed the club to Highbury, joining the board of directors and taking on the roles of secretary and then managing director.

Allison would win two league titles and one FA Cup as manager, but his style was very different to Chapman's. He was much less hands on and left the coaching and player interaction to Shaw and trainer Tom Whittaker, concentrating instead on transfer policy and media relations.

The outbreak of the Second World War in 1939 saw the suspension of national football competition but Allison remained in charge. After a disappointing thirteenth placed finish in 1946-47 when the Football League resumed he retired from the game and died in 1957.

1934
THE BATTLE
OF HIGHBURY

A record that still stands today was set on 14th November 1934 when seven players from the same club started an England match. The game against Italy, played at Arsenal's home stadium, became known as the Battle of Highbury.

Italy were the reigning world champions and the Arsenal players selected were Frank Moss, George Male, Eddie Hapgood, Wilf Copping, Ray Bowden, Ted Drake and Cliff Bastin. The Italians were reportedly offered an Alfa Romeo by Prime Minister Benito Mussolini if they won the game.

After just two minutes Italian defender Luis Monte broke his foot in a tough tackle on Drake but continued as there were no substitutes then. England took advantage of this to score three goals in ten minutes. Monte then went off, leading to the Italians changing their tactics and becoming more defensive. They also continued their rough treatment, leaving Hapgood with a broken nose and Eric Brook with a fractured arm.

The score remained 3-0 at halftime but Giuseppe Meazza scored twice in the first seventeen minutes after the break to bring it back to 3-2. Some great goalkeeping though from Moss allowed England to hold out. Due to the violent tactics of the Italians the FA considered stopping internationals altogether and the legendary Stanley Matthews later said it was the toughest game he ever played.

1935
A TITLE
HAT-TRICK

Arsenal achieved a title hat-trick in 1934-35, matching the achievement of Huddersfield the previous decade.

Centre forward Ted Drake was signed from Southampton before the season started and he would be a key figure of the campaign. He got seven hat-tricks and his final tally was 42 goals in 41 games. The Gunners were unstoppable at Highbury, where there were 8-0 wins over Leicester and Middlesbrough, while Liverpool were beaten 8-1. Tottenham were destroyed twice, with Arsenal winning 5-1 at Highbury and 6-0 at White Hart Lane.

Although Drake was the leading scorer others got their share. Cliff Bastin hit twenty and Ray Bowden got fourteen from just 24 games. In all, sixteen different players scored goals and even keeper Frank Moss got on the scoresheet in a 2-0 win at Everton. He had picked up an injury but had to go on the right wing as there were no substitutes allowed.

The Gunners went top of the table in January and stayed there, wrapping up the title with a 1-0 win at Middlesbrough on 22nd April, with two games still remaining. They finished the season four points clear of second placed Sunderland.

1935
TED DRAKE
SCORES SEVEN

A league goalscoring record that still stands today was set on 14th December 1935 when Ted Drake scored all of Arsenal's goals in a 7-1 win at Aston Villa. Going into the game Arsenal were fourth in the table, but eight points behind leaders Sunderland. Aston Villa were bottom but nobody could have foreseen what was to come, especially as Drake had his left knee bandaged due to an injury.

In front of over 60,000 fans, Villa were the better side early on but three classic counter attacking goals by Drake put Arsenal 3-0 up at halftime. He then completed his second hat-trick after just fifteen minutes of the second half, two of those goals coming when he seized on defensive mistakes.

Villa pulled one back through Palethorpe but in the final minute Drake got his seventh. He had only two other shots all game, one being saved and the other hitting the bar.

Drake's achievement set a new league goalscoring record and has not been matched in English top flight football. Ironically though, just twelve days after he got seven, Tranmere's Bunny Bell scored nine in their 13-4 win over Oldham.

At the end of the season Villa were relegated while Arsenal failed to secure a fourth successive title, finishing in sixth place.

1936
REPORTERS BANNED
AS ARSENAL WIN THE CUP

Arsenal won their second FA Cup in 1935-36 in a final where reporters were banned from Wembley in a dispute over costs.

The Gunners reached the final with wins over Bristol Rovers, Liverpool, Newcastle, Barnsley and Grimsby. They were clear favourites for the final, their opponents being 2nd Division Sheffield United.

Due to a disagreement over fees, the FA did not allow reporters into Wembley for the game. This led to many journalists hiring autogyros to fly above the stadium in a bid to report on the action.

United were the better side early on as Arsenal struggled to adapt to the windy conditions. Only poor finishing prevented Arsenal from falling behind and when they did manage to attack, Cliff Bastin was out of form.

Arsenal's defending did improve, restricting their opponents to long shots and the score remained 0-0 at halftime.

In the second half Arsenal improved and defender Jack Crayston was able to get forward to help the attack out. Bastin went close with a header and eventually their dominance was rewarded in the 74th minute. Bastin beat his man and crossed the ball for Ted Drake to score. There was a scare a few minutes after the goal when United hit the bar but Arsenal held on for victory.

1936
THE MARBLE HALLS

In 1936 Arsenal's stature in the game was emphasised with the opening of the East Stand, containing the Marble Halls.

The cantilevered West Stand, containing roomy seats opened in 1932 but it was the East Stand which really made a statement about the club. One of the two architects was Claude Ferrier, who included features in it from his native France.

The stand cost £130,000 to build, a huge sum at the time, as only the best would do when it came to the dressing rooms and club reception facilities. The baths were marble and there were even hospitality bars, unheard of at the time. The offices were oak panelled and the floors laid with Italian Terrazzo tiles. A bronze bust of Herbert Chapman, sculpted by Jacob Epstein, was also on display.

Outside, the facade was cream with Arsenal Stadium etched in huge letters as well as a cannon. Fans were protected from the elements not just by the roof but perspex screens at either side. They also had the luxury of proper toilets, as opposed to the troughs that they had previously been used to.

When Arsenal moved to the Emirates Stadium in 2006, the old ground was converted to an apartment complex called Highbury Square, the Marble Halls remaining as a reception area for the residents.

1937
THE FIRST LIVE
TELEVISED FOOTBALL MATCH

FACT **34**

The first football match to be televised live took place at Highbury on 16th September 1937, when Arsenal's first team and reserves played each other.

The BBC had begun its television service the previous year and this exhibition match at the nearest ground to their studios was arranged so they could demonstrate their ability to show live sport. They used three cameras, one placed in the stand and two near the goals. However they didn't show the whole game, just an introduction of the teams and the first few minutes.

It was a rainy day and as such the pictures on viewers' black and white television screens were quite dull. It was a useful exercise for the future, although the Football League had already made it known that they opposed the live transmission of games.

No record remains of the result of the game, which was played in an empty stadium. In fact it is unlikely that a full ninety minute contest took place. Arsenal had played at Bolton the day before and were due to face Sunderland two days later.

1938
FINAL DAY
TITLE SUCCESS

Arsenal won their fifth Football League Championship of the decade in 1937-38 but unlike in previous seasons, they didn't clinch the title until the final day.

Cliff Bastin and Ted Drake were again the main goalscoring threat in a season that saw Arsenal open with three straight wins. They tailed off though and were fourth at Christmas, four points behind surprise leaders Brentford. With six games remaining Arsenal were top, but three games without a win saw Wolverhampton Wanders overtake them.

Going into the last day of the season, Arsenal were in second place, a point behind Wolves but with a better goal average. The Gunners cruised to a 5-0 win over Bolton. There was a carnival atmosphere towards the end as news came through that Wolves had lost 1-0 at Sunderland in game that kicked off fifteen minutes earlier.

The final whistle saw the crowd invade the pitch but the players managed to make it to the tunnel with the exception of Eddie Hapgood, who was chaired off. The crowd then sang Auld Lang Syne and the National Anthem before the celebrations continued on the streets and in the pubs around the ground.

1939
THE ARSENAL
STADIUM MYSTERY

One of the first films in which football was a major theme was *The Arsenal Stadium Mystery*, released in 1939.

The film starred Leslie Banks and Greta Gynt and was based around a friendly match between Arsenal and a fictional team named Trojans XI. A Trojans player dies during the game and it is later found that he was poisoned, with police suspecting his teammates or a former mistress.

Interior scenes were filmed at Denham Studios while Highbury was used for the action shots, which came from a league match against Brentford on 6th May 1939. Brentford wore a special striped kit for the game with the reason that they were body doubles for Trojans only being unveiled later.

A number of Arsenal players starred as well as trainer Tom Whittaker, but only manager George Allison had a speaking part. He is seen in the dressing room telling the players that the opposition played a more attacking game than they did.

The culprit was revealed as the Trojans manager and it was intended to make a follow up, but the advent of the Second World War curtailed it.

1940
HIGHBURY BOMBED

During the Second World War Arsenal's Highbury Stadium suffered extensive bomb damage.

After the outbreak of war in 1939, 42 of the club's 44 professional players were drafted into the armed forces, as well as a number of administration staff. One player excused from military service was Cliff Bastin, who had defective hearing.

The Football League was suspended but regional competitions were allowed. The club relied largely on guest players, with home fixtures being held at White Hart Lane due to Highbury being used as a first aid training centre for Air Raid Precautions officers.

During an air raid by German bombers in 1940 the North Bank terrace was destroyed, with the South Stand also being damaged. Bastin recalled in his autobiography that one of the goalposts had caught fire. As well as the bomb damage at Highbury, the club's training ground was also hit.

On the pitch Arsenal were reasonably successful, winning the London League, Football League South and Football League South Cup. When the war ended in 1945, they returned to Highbury where the North Bank had been rebuilt but without a roof, which wasn't added until 1956.

1945
THE FOGGY FRIENDLY

When Arsenal entertained Russian side Dynamo Moscow at White Hart Lane in 1945 hardly anybody could see what was going on due to the fog.

To celebrate the end of the Second World War the Football Association invited Dynamo Moscow to play a number of friendlies in England. It was reported that they insisted on facing Arsenal, as not doing so when they were in London would be like going to Egypt and not seeing the pyramids.

Dynamo started their tour by drawing 3-3 with Chelsea and then thrashed Cardiff City 10-1. The game against Arsenal on 21st November 1945 would be at White Hart Lane as Highbury still hadn't been repaired after bomb damage. Due to some players still being in the armed forces, Stanley Matthews and Stan Mortensen guested for Arsenal in a game that attracted 55,000 fans.

Due to the thick fog the conditions were so farcical that the players could hardly see each other. Dynamo scored in the first minute but Arsenal hit back to lead 2-1, only for the Russians to equalise before half time. The second half was so bad that the *Daily Herald* reporter was unable to describe the goals although the game ended 4-3 to Dynamo.

1947
CLIFF BASTIN
RETIRES

FACT **39**

One of Arsenal's greatest ever players retired during the 1946-47 season, leaving behind a goalscoring record that would not be broken for fifty years.

Arsenal signed Cliff Bastin from Exeter City in 1929 when he was just seventeen years old. He made 21 appearances in his first season and was a virtual ever present during the glorious decade of the 1930s when he helped the club to five league titles and two FA Cups.

Bastin was the leading scorer in the title winning sides of 1933 and 1934 but after the arrival of Ted Drake he played a more withdrawn role. He was first and foremost a creator of goals but also chipped in with a number himself.

After missing much of 1938-39 through injury the outbreak of the Second World War disrupted his career. He appeared in wartime fixtures, but his leg injury continued to hinder him. When the Football League resumed in 1946-47 Bastin continued to struggle and played only seven times without scoring before deciding to retire in January 1947.

Bastin's total of 178 goals was not surpassed until 1997 when Ian Wright overtook him, with Thierry Henry knocking him down to third place in 2005. Had the war not intervened though, he might have set a record that neither Wright or Henry could have broken.

1948
POST WAR
TITLE SUCCESS

After a disappointing return to Football League action after the Second World War, Arsenal bounced back in 1947-48 to win their sixth league title.

The Gunners finished in thirteenth place in 1946-47, sixteen points behind champions Liverpool. George Allison retired as manager and was replaced by trainer Tom Whittaker.

Arsenal got off to a perfect start, winning their first six games and remaining unbeaten until the end of November when they lost 1-0 at Derby in their eighteenth fixture.

There was a shock defeat to Bradford Park Avenue in the FA Cup 3rd round but the title never looked in doubt. The following week The Gunners drew 1-1 at Manchester United in front of a crowd of 83,260, still a record in English league football.

That draw kept Arsenal five points clear of nearest challengers Burnley. After such an excellent start they were never off the top of the table all season thanks in part to the goals of Ronnie Rooke, who was the 1st Division's leading scorer with 33.

The title was secured with a 1-1 draw at Huddersfield on 10th April when there were still four games left to play. They failed to win any of the next three but rounded the season off in style at Highbury on 1st May, beating Grimsby Town 8-0.

1950
LOSERS MEDAL FOR
CUP WINNING CAPTAIN

When Joe Mercer captained Arsenal to FA Cup success in 1950 he was handed a losers medal in error by the queen.

Mercer, who played on the left of midfield, had signed for Arsenal in 1946 from Everton and took over the captaincy in 1948. What was remarkable about Mercer's playing career with Arsenal was that he continued to live and train on Merseyside as he had business interests in the area.

Arsenal's opponents in the cup final would be Liverpool, who sportingly let him train at their facilities, but made sure he couldn't see what tactics they were preparing for the big day.

On a rainy day at Wembley Reg Lewis gave Arsenal a seventeenth minute lead, but Liverpool fought back and Albert Stubbins twice went close with headers. Mercer and Alex Forbes did a great job of snuffing out Liverpool attacks and shortly after the hour Mark Lewis added a second, capping a great counter attacking move.

When Mercer climbed the steps to receive the cup from Queen Elizabeth he was given a losers medal by mistake, but this was rectified before he returned to the pitch. He remained at the club for a further four years and after retiring managed Sheffield United, Manchester City, Aston Villa and Coventry City.

1951
FLOODLIGHTS COME
TO HIGHBURY

Arsenal were one of the first English clubs to install floodlights with the ground being illuminated for the first time in September 1951.

Herbert Chapman was impressed when he saw floodlights in Belgium in the 1930s and installed them at Arsenal's training ground. The Football League resisted any calls to play matches under them though and it wasn't until 1950 that Southampton became the first club to install them at a ground.

The following year both Arsenal and Tottenham

erected floodlights and Israeli side Hapoel Tel Aviv were invited to play a friendly at Highbury to celebrate the switch on.

Newspapers reported that the 84 lamps, each with 1500 watts of power, allowed spectators a 'splendid view' and that the white ball was 'easily followed'.

Arsenal dominated the game with Cliff Holton scoring a hat-trick in 6-1 win. Four weeks later Glasgow Rangers came to Highbury and were beaten 3-2, while in 1952 Hibernian were thrashed 7-1 in a televised floodlit friendly.

Competitive games under floodlights were finally allowed by the football authorities in 1956 and in 1962 new ones were installed at Highbury, the original set being sold to Irish club Bohemians for their Dalymount Park ground.

1952
DOUBLE
DISAPPOINTMENT

Arsenal were left disappointed in 1951-52 when they blew the league title at the last hurdle and then lost the FA Cup final.

With two league games remaining the Gunners were second in the table, only behind leaders Manchester United on goal average. With Arsenal due to face United on the last day of the season the title was in their own hands but in the penultimate game they were beaten 3-1 by West Bromwich Albion.

The defeat to Albion meant that in the final game Arsenal had to beat Manchester United 7-0 at Old Trafford to turn the goal average around and be crowned champions. There was never even a glimmer of hope as the Gunners were thrashed 6-1 and ended up third in the table, being overtaken by Tottenham.

On 3rd May Arsenal faced Newcastle in the FA Cup final at Wembley. They were dealt a blow after 35 minutes when Wally Barnes twisted his knee and had to go off. With no substitutes allowed this meant Arsenal having to carry on with ten men.

In the second half Cliff Holton, Don Roper and Ray Daniel all struggled with injury but Newcastle were unable to make this advantage count. Eventually with six minutes left their Chilean striker Jorge Robledo scored, leaving the Gunners empty handed.

1953
CHAMPIONS ON
GOAL AVERAGE

After the disappointment of the previous season, Arsenal clinched a record breaking seventh league title in their last game of 1952-53, pipping Preston on goal average.

The Gunners won only four of their first ten games but began to really hit form at the beginning of November. A 2-1 win over Middesbrough at Highbury on the 8th of the month was the first of seven games unbeaten. A thrilling 6-4 win at Bolton on Christmas Day meant they were second going into New Year, a point behind Wolves with a game in hand.

In January Wolves were beaten 5-3 and there was a 4-0 win over Tottenham at Highbury the following month. In April five straight wins took Arsenal to the brink of glory and they knew victory at Preston in the penultimate game would secure the title. They were beaten 2-0, which allowed Preston to draw level on points but Arsenal had the better goal average.

In their last game Arsenal took on Burnley at Highbury, knowing only victory would do as Preston had moved two points clear with victory in their final match. Burnley took an early lead but Arsenal came back to win 3-2, meaning they had now won more league titles than any other English side.

1956
DEATH OF
TOM WHITTAKER

Arsenal Football Club was stunned in 1956 when manager Tom Whittaker died of a heart attack.

Whittaker's playing career had been cut short in 1925 when he suffered a serious knee injury. He then studied physiotherapy and became Arsenal's physio and trainer, taking over from George Allison as manager in 1947.

After leading Arsenal to two titles and two FA Cups he struggled to replace players of the calibre of Cliff Bastin and Joe Mercer in the mid 1950s. The maximum wage meant it was far harder to persuade players to move and an audacious bid for Stanley Matthews failed.

As well as overseeing team affairs, Whittaker was the club secretary and responsible for many administrative tasks, even handling season ticket sales. The strain began to show and on 24th October 1956, when Arsenal were way down the table in eleventh place, he was taken to University College Hospital with a suspected heart attack. He died later that day at the age of just 58.

Whittaker was a man who had fought in both world wars without getting wounded, but in the end it was football that killed him. His assistant Jack Crayston replaced him on a caretaker basis and the appointment was made permanent in December.

1958
THE BUSBY BABES
LAST LEAGUE MATCH

One of the most thrilling games ever seen at Highbury was also the last time the famous Busby Babes played on English soil.

The Busby Babes were a nickname given to Manchester United's young stars, who had won the league title two years running by using an exciting attacking style of play.

Their visit to Highbury on 1st February 1958 attracted 63,000 fans. They took Arsenal apart in the first half and led 3-0 at the break thanks to goals from Duncan Edwards, Bobby Charlton and Tommy Taylor.

In the second half Arsenal struck back and unbelievably scored three times in three minutes to level it at 3-3. David Herd started the comeback and Jimmy Bloomfield got two, the second a magnificent diving header. However United went further ahead thanks to goals from Dennis Viollett and Taylor. Derek Tapscott pulled it back to 5-4 and Vic Groves missed a great chance to equalise but United held on.

It would be the last time this United side played on English soil. Five days later their plane crashed in Munich on the way home from a European Cup tie. Five of the side who had played at Highbury, including goalscorers Edwards and Taylor, were killed.

1962
BILLY WRIGHT'S
ARRIVAL

Arsenal broke with tradition in 1962 when they appointed a manager who had no connection to the club. However one of the greatest players in the game did not prove to be a managerial success.

After Tom Whittaker's death Jack Crayston was in charge until 1958 and was replaced by former player George Swindin. He had won three Midland League titles with Peterborough and taken them on an FA Cup run to the fourth round.

Swindin resigned in 1962 and was replaced by Wright, a former England captain who had played his whole career at Wolverhampton, where he won three league titles and an FA Cup. He was the first Arsenal manager to be appointed since Herbert Chapman who had no previous connection to the club.

Wright's first season was a reasonable one that saw the club finish seventh and qualify for Europe for the first time. However things gradually declined and Wright was sacked after finishing fourteenth in 1966. Statistically, he has the worst record of Arsenal managers since the Second World War, with the exception of caretaker managers.

Wright never managed again, instead working in television. He died of pancreatic cancer in 1994 at the age of seventy.

Arsenal's first appearance in European competition came in 1963 when they qualified for the Fairs Cup, a forerunner of the Europa League.

After finishing seventh in the league table, Arsenal were one of two English representatives in the competition, the other being Sheffield Wednesday.

In the first round Arsenal were paired with Danish side Staevnet, who they thrashed 7-1 away from home. John MacLeod scored the club's first European goal after ten minutes of a game which Arsenal led 5-0 at halftime. Geoff Strong and Joe Baker both got hat-tricks, with Staevnet's goal coming nine minutes from time.

In the return leg at Highbury Alan Skirton gave Arsenal a first minute lead but the expected goal avalanche never came and the Danes came back from 2-1 down in the second half to win 3-2.

Arsenal were drawn against Belgian side FC Liege in the second round. The first leg at Highbury ended in a 1-1 draw, Terry Anderson equalising in the second half after the Gunners had trailed at halftime.

In Liege Billy McCullough gave Arsenal the lead after half an hour but Liege struck twice in a minute to lead 2-1 at the break. Midway through the second half Liege scored again to end Arsenal's hopes of progress and it would be another six years before they were back in Europe.

1965
THE SEVENTEEN YEAR OLD
HAT-TRICK HERO

In January 1965 John Radford hit a hat-trick against Wolverhampton Wanderers at Highbury, setting a record that still stands today.

Radford joined Arsenal as an apprentice in 1962 and turned professional on his seventeenth birthday in February 1964. He was aged seventeen years and 315 days when he was selected to face Wolves on 2nd January 1965, only his third appearance for the first team.

Wolves took a tenth minute lead but this was soon cancelled out when the powerfully built Radford headed in a Joe Baker cross for his first ever Arsenal goal. His second was a tap in from a few yards when he seized on a mistake by the Wolves' keeper.

Baker made it 3-1 before half time and the second half was largely uneventful. However with two minutes left Alan Skirton went on a great run down the left wing and cut into the box, then unselfishly passed to Radford who completed his hat-trick.

Radford's record of being the youngest Arsenal player to score a hat-trick has not been broken. He remained at Arsenal until 1976, finishing his career with 149 goals in 481 appearances.

1966
BERTIE MEE
BECOMES MANAGER

After four mediocre years under Billy Wright Arsenal went back to tradition in 1966 when they appointed a new manager from within.

The brush with relegation in 1965-66 led to Wright's dismissal and the directors appointed physio Bertie Mee, who had been at Highbury since 1960. Mee was not even sure himself if he was the right person. He only accepted the job on the proviso he could return to being the club physio after a year if it didn't work out.

Knowing that the job was too big for him on his own, Mee made tow astute appointments to work alongside him. Leyton Orient manager Dave Sexton was brought in as his assistant and when he left the following year, reserve team coach Don Howe was promoted to assistant manager.

Mee would go on to enjoy great success with Arsenal, getting the best out of players such as John Radford, Frank McLintock and Bob Wilson who had been given a chance by Wright. After leaving the club in 1976 he never managed anyone else, instead working at Watford as an assistant to Graham Taylor and as a scout.

1966
HIGHBURY'S
LOWEST ATTENDANCE

51

As the disappointing 1965-66 season drew to a close Arsenal played Leeds in front of just 4,554 spectators, the lowest crowd to watch a first team fixture at Highbury.

Since the New Year Arsenal had been in freefall. They had won just two out of sixteen games in the league, both away from home. Fans at home games were making their discontent known and after a 3-1 defeat to Newcastle, just 8,738 turned up for the next home game against West Bromwich Albion.

The low point came on a Thursday night at the beginning of May. In Arsenal's penultimate home game of the season, only 4,554 fans came to Highbury to see the Gunners take on second paced Leeds United. It was another disappointing performance as Leeds cruised to a 3-0 win although they had no chance of catching Liverpool, who had already clinched the championship.

There were some other mitigating factors as to why the crowd was so low. It was a cold wet night and the European Cup Winners Cup final was being shown live on television. Two days later the season came to a close as Arsenal finally won at home, 1-0 against Leicester City, in front of 16,441 fans.

1969
FLU HIT SQUAD LOSE
LEAGUE CUP FINAL

Arsenal suffered a shock defeat to 3rd Division Swindon Town in the 1968-69 League Cup final. However their preparations were not helped when the squad were hit by a flu bug.

This was Arsenal's second successive League Cup final, having lost to Leeds United the previous year. They were clear favourites to beat Swindon, but preparations were hampered when eight players were struck down with flu. This caused the postponement of the match the week before the final.

The pitch at Wembley was also not in the best condition after hosting the Horse of the Year Show the same week. This meant Arsenal could not play their usual short passing game as much as they liked, but they still dominated the first half. However against the run of play Swindon took the lead in the 35th minute after a defensive mix-up between Bob Wilson and Ian Ure.

Arsenal dominated the second half but couldn't find an equaliser until Bobby Gould headed home in the 86th minute. In extra time though the Gunners were drained, the heavy pitch taking its toll on players still shaking off the effects of flu. Swindon scored twice to claim the trophy but Arsenal had just one more year to wait for the good times to return.

1970
EUROPEAN
TRIUMPH

Arsenal won their first trophy in seventeen years on 28th April 1970, lifting the UEFA Fairs Cup in only their second European season.

The Gunners qualified for the Fairs Cup after finishing 4th in 1968-69. They then beat Glentoran, Sporting Lisbon, Charleroi, Rhouen, Dinamo Bacau and Ajax to reach the final against Belgian side Anderlecht.

The final was a two leg affair but it looked all but over when Arsenal went 3-0 down in the first leg in Brussels. However a crucial away goal by Ray Kennedy eight minutes from time gave them some hope for the return leg.

Six days later at Highbury a crowd of 51,612 saw a cagey opening to the game, but things sprung to life after 25 minutes when Eddie Kelly hit a great strike from outside the box.

In the second half there was a scare when Jan Mulder hit the post but John Radford's 75th minute header levelled the scores on aggregate. Just a minute later Jon Sammels made it 3-0 to seal victory for The Gunners.

The cup was handed to captain Frank McLintock by FIFA chairman Sir Stanley Rous and a number of fans ran onto the pitch and joined the players for a lap of honour.

1971
WINNING THE LEAGUE
AT TOTTENHAM

FACT **54**

When Arsenal won the League Championship in 1970-71, they clinched the title with a victory at White Hart Lane.

The race went right down to the wire and Arsenal's final game on 3rd May 1971 was a rearranged fixture away to rivals Tottenham. Trailing Leeds by one point, The Gunners knew a win or 0-0 draw would be enough to clinch the title.

There were over 51,000 inside the ground and it was estimated that twice that many were locked out. Martin Peters nearly scored for Spurs early on but Arsenal settled and Charlie George and George Graham both went close.

With three minutes remaining John Radford's shot was saved but the ball was chipped back into the danger area by George Armstrong. Ray Kennedy met the cross with a powerful header that bounced into the goal off the underside of the bar.

Due to the goal average situation, a 1-1 draw would mean that Leeds would be champions. Kennedy later described it as the longest three minutes of his life but as Spurs pressed forward, Bob Wilson kept a cool head in goal.

Arsenal had won their eighth title and just five days later they would complete a remarkable double.

1971
THE DOUBLE

Just five days after the famous win at Tottenham, Arsenal became only the second team of the 20th Century to win the Double of League Championship and FA Cup in the same season.

On a really hot day Liverpool started off better but as the first half went on Arsenal created some useful chances only to be denied by Reds' keeper Ray Clemence. The second half was played at a slower pace with Arsenal's best chance coming when George Graham headed against the bar.

The game went into extra time and in the first minute Steve Heighway scored for Liverpool. The Reds then pressed for a second goal with Wilson making a great reflex save from John Toshack. Four minutes from the break Arsenal equalised when Liverpool's defence failed to clear a John Radford overhead kick and Liam Kelly prodded the ball into the net.

By the second period of extra time players on both sides were beginning to struggle with cramp and the number of errors increased. In the seventh minute Charlie George got the ball outside the box and hit an unstoppable shot into the top corner of the goal, then celebrated by famously lying on his back.

There were few more chances for either side and Arsenal had now emulated Spurs achievement of ten years earlier by winning the Double.

1973
LIAM BRADY'S
DEBUT

One of Arsenal's greatest ever players made his debut as a seventeen year old substitute against Birmingham City on 6th October 1973.

Raised in Dublin, Liam Brady signed schoolboy forms with Arsenal aged fifteen and turned professional on 13th February 1973, his seventeenth birthday. His debut was a sound one but in his first start against Tottenham he was disappointing and he appeared only occasionally for the rest of that 1973-74 season.

In 1974-75 Brady became a regular and for the next three seasons starred in a side that struggled in the middle or bottom half of the table. Towards the end of the 1970s Arsenal improved after Terry Neill's appointment as manager and they reached three successive FA Cup finals. Brady's close control of the ball and excellent passing ability made him the perfect creator of chances for the front men.

Brady was the club's player of the year three times and won the Professional Football Association player of the award in 1979. However in 1980 he wanted a new challenge and moved to Juventus in Italy where he won two Serie A titles.

After retiring from playing in 1990, Brady managed Brighton and Celtic before joining Arsenal as head of youth development in 1996. He stayed in that role for eighteen years and then became a club ambassador.

1976
ARSENAL'S
YOUNGEST MANAGER

When Bertie Mee left the club in 1976 he was replaced by former Arsenal defender Terry Neill, becoming the club's youngest manager at the age of just 34 years old.

A defender as a player, Neill had joined Arsenal in 1959 and remained at the club until 1970, leaving to become player manager at Hull City. He then managed Tottenham for two years, narrowly avoiding relegation in his first season but improving to finish ninth in his second.

Before making a move for Neill, Arsenal had made an audacious bid to lure Milan Milanic away from Real Madrid at a time when foreign managers were unheard of in English football.

Neill promised Arsenal's supporters that they would see an attacking brand of football. The signing of striker Malcolm MacDonald from Newcastle showed the club's ambition and he also brought in keeper Pat Jennings from his old club Tottenham.

Neill was at Arsenal for seven years, taking them to three successive FA Cup finals. In 1981 they were third in the league, their highest finish for ten years. However some high profile signings failed to live up to expectations and after a disappointing start to 1983-84 Neill was sacked.

Following his dismissal Neill retired from football and went into the pub business and also worked in the media.

1977
THE WORST
LEAGUE RUN

The worst losing run in Arsenal's history came in 1976-77 when seven successive defeats ended their hopes of winning the league.

At the end of the 1976 Arsenal were in sixth place, seven points behind leaders Liverpool but with three games in hand. They then won only one of four league games in January, drawing two and losing the other.

On 12th February they were beaten 1-0 at Manchester City then three days later lost 3-0 at Middlesbrough. A 3-2 home defeat by West Ham followed, then they lost 2-1 against Everton at Goodison Park. Ipswich then comfortably won 4-1 at Highbury and in the next home game, just 19,517 turned up to see West Bromwich Albion win 3-1. The seventh successive loss was at Loftus Road, where QPR won 2-1.

During the losing run Arsenal were also dumped out of the FA Cup by Middlesbrough, who beat them 4-1 at Ayresome Park making it eight successive defeats in all competitions. The run finally came to an end on 23rd March with a 1-1 draw at Stoke. The following week, fans finally witnessed a win when Leicester were beaten 1-0 at Highbury, bringing to an end an eleven game winless run.

1978
TOTTENHAM 0
ARSENAL 5

One of Arsenal's greatest games against their biggest rivals came two days before Christmas in 1978 when they won 5-0 at White Hart Lane.

Spurs had pulled off a transfer coup in the summer by signing two Argentine World Cup winning stars, Ricky Villa and Osvaldo Ardiles. However they were outshone by Liam Brady, who put in a stunning performance.

Arsenal went in front in the first minute when a bizarre backpass from the halfway line by John Pratt was latched onto by Alan Sunderland to score. In the 38th minute Sunderland got another with a left foot drive from the edge of the area after Brady had played him a brilliant pass from the halfway line.

Just after the hour Brady crossed from the left to Frank Stapleton, who volleyed home from inside the six yard box to make it 3-0. Four minutes later Brady dispossessed Peter Taylor and scored with a brilliant curling shot from outside the box.

The fifth goal in the 82nd minute was classic route one stuff. Pat Jennings's long goal kick was headed on by Stapleton to Sunderland who burst into the area and completed his hat-trick.

The result remains Arsenal's best win at White Hart Lane since the Second World War. The Gunners finished the season in seventh place, while Spurs were eleventh.

1979
THE FIVE MINUTE
FINAL

Arsenal won their first trophy for eight years in an FA Cup final that came to life in the last five minutes.

The Gunners had surprisingly been beaten by Ipswich in the previous year's final at Wembley and now faced a Manchester United side looking to repeat their success of two years earlier.

Brian Talbot put the Gunners ahead in the twelfth minute when he scored from close range. Two minutes from halftime Frank Stapleton made it 2-0, heading in Liam Brady's cross.

The second half was largely uneventful and as the game entered the last five minutes there was little indication of what was to come. Gordon McQueen stabbed the ball home to pull one back then two minutes later Sammy McIlroy equalised to stun the Arsenal players and support.

Extra time looked inevitable but a minute after McIlroy's goal Brady released Graham Rix down the left wing. He hit a curling cross into the box which keeper Gary Bailey failed to reach and Alan Sunderland slid in at the far post to score the winner. There was no way back for United now and Arsenal captain Pat Rice collected the cup from Prince Charles.

1980
THE 70 GAME
SEASON

In 1979-80 Arsenal played a record breaking seventy games in all competitions, a record unlikely to be broken.

Arsenal played 42 games in the league and finished fourth. They never really looked like challenging Liverpool for the title and excelled in the cups instead.

Defending the FA Cup, Arsenal needed replays to get past Cardiff in the 3rd round and Bolton in the 5th round. In the semi-final though, they endured a mammoth tie against Liverpool, which was finally settled in a third replay at Coventry after one 0-0 and two 1-1 draws.

In between the first and second games against Liverpool, Arsenal travelled to Turin for the second leg of the European Cup Winners Cup semi-final. With two minutes remaining Arsenal looked to be on their way out due to the away goals rule, but teenage substitute Paul Vaessen headed a goal to take The Gunners to the final.

On 10th May Arsenal faced 2nd Division West Ham in the FA Cup final at Wembley and surprisingly lost 1-0. Four days later they were in Brussels to play Valencia in the Cup Winners Cup final. The game ended 0-0 and they then lost the penalty shoot out.

After seventy games Arsenal had ended up with no reward. Remarkably Brian Talbot started every game, being substituted only twice.

1983
CHARLIE NICHOLAS

In the summer of 1983 Arsenal were involved in one of their most exciting transfers ever when British football's hottest young talent arrived at Highbury.

21 year old Charlie Nicholas scored 48 goals for Celtic in 1982-83 and was widely expected to join champions Liverpool, but he rejected them and Manchester United in favour of a move to North London. The fee was £750,000 and Nicholas reportedly became Britain's highest paid footballer.

Nicholas scored his first Arsenal goals in his second game, netting twice in a 2-1 win at Wolverhampton Wanderers. He then endured a barren spell and didn't find the net again until Boxing Day, when he scored twice in a 4-2 win at Tottenham. By now Don Howe was manager and Nicholas finished the season with eleven league goals.

Flamboyant Nicholas showed some great skills, but he was also inconsistent. However he did rise to the occasion in the 1987 League Cup final when he scored both goals in a 2-1 win over Liverpool.

When Alan Smith arrived in the summer of 1987 Nicholas was dropped and also found himself behind new talent Perry Groves. In January 1988 he returned to Scotland to join Aberdeen and later went back to Celtic. He now works in the media.

1985
PAT JENNINGS
RETIRES

One of the few players to transcend the North London rivalry retired from club football in 1985, having made over 1,000 senior appearances in his career.

Goalkeeper Pat Jennings joined Arsenal from Tottenham following their relegation in 1977 with their manager Keith Burkinshaw believing he was nearing the end of his career. He was Arsenal's first choice keeper for the next six seasons, helping them to four cup finals.

In 1982 George Wood arrived and became number

one but Jennings regained his place and stayed as first choice keeper until 1985. On 26th February 1983 he played his 1,000th senior game in a 0-0 draw at West Bromwich Albion.

Jennings left Arsenal having made 327 appearances for the Gunners. However his footballing career wasn't over. He remained Northern Ireland's first choice keeper and helped them qualify for the 1986 World Cup in Mexico. To maintain his fitness he trained with Spurs and played for their reserves, then ended his career by playing in the World Cup at the age of forty.

Jennings now works as a matchday host at White Hart Lane, but he has that special talent and personality to remain a hero to Arsenal fans as well.

1987
LEAGUE CUP
COMEBACK KINGS

When Arsenal won the League Cup in 1987 they did it the hard way, coming from behind twice against Tottenham in the semi-final, then against Liverpool at Wembley.

In the first leg of the semi-final Arsenal lost 1-0 against Tottenham at White Hart Lane. In the second leg at Highbury Spurs led 1-0 at halftime but second half goals from Viv Anderson and Niall Quinn levelled the tie. There were no away goals or penalties in the competition then and Spurs won the coin toss to decide the venue for the replay.

At White Hart Lane Arsenal trailed with ten minutes to go but Ian Allinson got an equaliser. Then with just two minutes remaining, David Rocastle got the winning goal to take Arsenal to Wembley.

Things didn't look good for the Gunners when Ian Rush gave Liverpool a 23rd minute lead in the final. The Reds had never lost in any of the 144 games in which Rush had scored for them, but Charlie Nicholas gave Arsenal hope with an equaliser on the half hour.

The game looked destined for extra time but with seven minutes left Perry Groves broke clear and set up Nicholas for his second goal. Arsenal then held on for their first trophy since 1979.

1987
14 CONSECUTIVE WINS

In 1987-88 Arsenal won fourteen successive games but still finished the season empty handed.

The run started on 12th September when the Gunners won 1-0 at Nottingham Forest, which was followed a week later with a 3-0 home win over Wimbledon.

The next three league games were all won without conceding a goal and during this run clean sheets were also kept in a 4-0 aggregate win over Doncaster in a two legged League Cup second round tie.

Arsenal finally conceded a goal at Tottenham on 18th October, but still came away with a 2-1 victory. They then beat Derby 2-1 at Highbury before a 3-0 home win over Bournemouth in the League Cup.

The league run continued with a 1-0 win at Newcastle, which was followed by a 3-1 home defeat of Chelsea and a 4-2 victory at Norwich. The fourteenth game saw a 3-0 home win over Stoke City in the League Cup.

Arsenal's winning streak finally came to an end on 21st November when Southampton won 1-0 at Highbury. The exceptional run had taken the Gunners to the top of the league, but Liverpool were just a point behind due to their own unbeaten start to the season. The Gunners would go on to finish sixth in the table and lost the League Cup final to Luton.

1988
TONY ADAMS
BECOMES CAPTAIN

One of Arsenal's greatest servants was appointed club captain in 1988 at the age of just 21.

One club man Tony Adams had made his debut just four weeks after his seventeenth birthday in November 1983. He matured over the next few years and George Graham had no qualms about appointing the defender as his next captain

Adams led Arsenal to their first title success for eighteen years in 1989 and was dubbed a Colossus by George Graham. A cruel tabloid headline in 1989 after scoring at both ends against Manchester United led to many jibes from opposition fans, but he always rose above them. His increasing medal haul was his way of responding to the taunts.

Although a defender, he scored some crucial goals, including an FA Cup semi-final winner against Tottenham in 1993 and the following year he got the decisive goal in the European Cup Winners Cup quarter-final against Torino. In the final of that competition he was a rock at the back as Arsenal triumphed over Parma.

There were further triumphs in 1998 and 2002, Adams leading Arsenal to the Double on each occasion. He then retired from playing, having played 669 games for the club and scoring 48 goals.

1989
IT'S UP FOR
GRABS NOW

In one of the most dramatic finishes to an English league campaign, Arsenal snatched the title in the closing seconds of the 1988-89 season.

With three games left the Gunners looked set for their first title since 1971. However, just one point from their final two home games handed the initiative to rivals Liverpool, who won their penultimate game to move three points clear.

The last game of the season would see Arsenal face the Reds at Anfield. A two goal victory would clinch the title for the Gunners but Liverpool hadn't lost by that margin at home for three years.

The first half was a tense affair with few chances, then seven minutes after the break Alan Smith scored with a glancing header from Nigel Winterburn's free kick to give the Gunners hope. Arsenal continued to attack but couldn't find that decisive goal.

In the second minute of injury time one last assault by Arsenal saw Lee Dixon's long ball flicked on by Smith. Michael Thomas took it into the area and as ITV commentator Brian Moore said 'It's up for grabs now' he coolly slipped the ball past keeper Bruce Grobbelaar.

The goal sparked wild celebrations amongst Arsenal's players and support. Arsenal were presented with the trophy after the game and sportingly applauded by the home crowd.

1990
RECORD FEE FOR
A GOALKEEPER

Arsenal smashed the British transfer record for a goalkeeper in the summer of 1990 season and it proved a sound investment.

It took a huge offer of £1.3 million to persuade QPR to part with England international David Seaman but George Graham's judgement was proved right when he conceded just eighteen goals as the Gunners won the league in 1990-91.

Seaman was the last line of one of the country's meanest defences and further glory followed with FA Cup and League Cup success in 1993 and the Cup Winners Cup in 1994.

Seaman remained the club's first choice keeper after Arsene Wenger's arrival in 1996 and when Arsenal won the league in 1997-98, he let in only seventeen goals. They won the Double that season and when they repeated the feat in 2001-02 he crucially saved a penalty in a 2-1 win at Aston Villa.

In the 2002-03 FA Cup semi-final, Seaman played his 1000th career game and made arguably his best ever save, diving across the goal to scoop away Paul Peschisolido's header. He was named captain for the final against Southampton, lifting the cup after a 1-0 win.

That summer at the age of 39, Seaman left Arsenal and joined Manchester City, but in January 2004 he announced his retirement due to a shoulder injury.

1991
HANDED
THE TITLE

George Graham's second league title triumph wasn't quite as dramatic as two years earlier. Arsenal's last home game was a title party thanks to Liverpool's defeat earlier in the day.

The Gunners and the Reds pulled away from the rest of the pack from the start, both enjoying fourteen game unbeaten starts. On 2nd December 1990 Arsenal beat Liverpool 3-0 at Highbury and they were not beaten in the league until their 25th game.

Arsenal beat Liverpool 1-0 in a crunch encounter at Anfield on 3rd March to go top on goal difference but it was over the Easter weekend when they really seized the initiative. They moved five points clear by winning twice while Liverpool could only pick up one point from their games.

Going into the final week of the season Arsenal knew that one win from their last two games would seal the title. On 6th May Liverpool lost 2-1 at Nottingham Forest in a 5pm kick off, watched by Arsenal's players on television as they prepared to face Manchester United at 8pm.

The Gunners had been handed the title and they were then given a guard of honour by United's players, before beating them 3-1 in a carnival atmosphere. The following Saturday the players received the trophy after a 6-1 win over Coventry.

1992
THE END OF
THE NORTH BANK

The last game in front of the famous North Bank terrace saw Ian Wright clinch the Golden Boot for being the 1st Division's leading scorer.

The introduction of all seater stadia meant that the terrace which had stood since 1913 and been the home of Arsenal's most vociferous support had to be replaced with an all seater stand.

Arsenal rarely looked like retaining the title, being twenty points behind leaders Manchester United at the end of January. They rallied and were unbeaten for the remainder of the season, but they could only finish fourth.

As injury time approached in the last game in front of the North Bank against Southampton on 2nd May, the Gunners were cruising to a routine 3-1 win. However the Golden Boot looked to be on its way to Gary Lineker, who was one goal ahead of Wright.

There was little indication of the drama that would unfold when David Seaman found Wright with a long throw, but the striker beat off his challengers to score. Then with Arsenal's last attack Wright turned in a cross to make it 5-1 and snatch the Golden Boot from Lineker in dramatic fashion.

That summer the North Bank was demolished and for 1992-93 a mural stood behind the goal while the new 12,000 seat stand was being built.

1993
DOUBLE CUP
WINNERS

In 1992-93 Arsenal became the first team to win the League and FA Cups in the same season.

The Gunners were again disappointing in the league, finishing tenth in the newly formed Premiership. However there was no repeat of the previous year's cup upset, when the Gunners lost 2-1 at 4th Division Wrexham.

In the League Cup second round they beat Millwall on penalties after two 1-1 draws, then knocked out Derby after a replay. A potential upset was avoided with a 1-0 win at Scarborough, then Nottingham Forest were beaten at Highbury in the fifth round.

The semi-final saw a comfortable 5-1 aggregate win over Crystal Palace. In the final against Sheffield Wednesday Arsenal came back from 1-0 down to win 2-1 thanks to goals from Paul Merson and Steve Morrow, who broke his arm in the post-match celebrations falling from Tony Adams's shoulders.

In the FA Cup there were wins over Yeovil, Leeds, Nottingham Forest and Ipswich to set up a semi-final with Tottenham at Wembley, which the Gunners won 1-0.

Sheffield Wednesday were again the opponents for the final and the game ended 1-1. The replay looked set to finish 1-1 too as the end of extra time approached. However, with penalties looming Andy Linighan rose to head in a Merson corner to make cup history.

1993
DAVID O'LEARY
LEAVES

The end of the 1992-93 season saw Arsenal's record appearance holder leave for pastures new.

Born in London but raised in Dublin, David O'Leary joined the club as an apprentice in 1973. He made his debut aged just seventeen in the first game of 1975-76 away at Burnley and played thirty times that season.

For the next decade O'Leary rarely missed a match at centre back, playing with composure and having an excellent ability to read the game. He was also extremely strong for someone of such slim build. Unlike some of the club's other top names, O'Leary stayed at Highbury in the difficult years of the early to mid 1980s and enjoyed League Cup success in 1987.

By the time of the 1989 and 1991 league title triumphs though he was no longer first choice thanks to the pairing of Tony Adams and Steve Bould.

O'Leary's professionalism and willingness to play where and when required meant he continued to have a role under George Graham and he came on as a substitute in the 1993 FA Cup final and replay.

In the close season though he left on a free transfer for Leeds United, who he later managed. In total he played 722 games for Arsenal, a record that nobody else has matched.

1994
A SECOND
EUROPEAN TROPHY

Arsenal achieved European glory for the second time in 1993-94 when they won the European Cup Winners Cup.

In the first round Arsenal were paired with Danish side Odense, who took a shock lead in the first leg in Denmark. The Gunners came back to win 2-1, then drew 1-1 at Highbury to progress to the next round where they were drawn against Belgium's Standard Liege.

In the first leg against the Belgians at Highbury Arsenal won 3-0 and in Liege they as good as sealed progress in the second minute when Alan Smith scored. The Gunners didn't sit back though and went on to hammer the home side 7-0.

Arsenal then faced a tough quarter-final with Torino, UEFA Cup finalists two years earlier. After a 0-0 draw in Turin, Tony Adams's goal was enough to take the Gunners to the semi-final and a tie against Paris Saint Germain. A 1-1 draw in Paris was followed by another 1-0 win at Highbury, setting up a final with Italian side Parma in Copenhagen.

Parma were defending the trophy and Arsenal were without the suspended Ian Wright. However Smith's 22nd minute goal was enough to win the trophy for Arsenal who defended resolutely throughout the game. The Gunners became the fourth London club to win the competition.

1994
JOHN JENSEN
SCORES

On New Year's Eve 1994 Arsenal cult figure John Jensen scored his only goal for the club.

A Danish international midfielder, Jensen arrived at Highbury in the summer of 1992. Fresh from scoring in Denmark's unlikely triumph over Germany in the European Championship final, he was seen by some as a replacement for the popular David Rocastle who had been sold to champions Leeds.

Over the next few seasons Jensen worked hard but his failure to find the net became something of a joke amongst supporters. His goal against Germany was all most fans had seen of him before his arrival and as time went on cries of 'shoot' got louder every time he got the ball.

Finally, in his 98th game for the club, Jensen's moment came on 31st December 1994 at home to Queens Park Rangers. Collecting the ball on the edge of the area, he curled a shot into the top corner to the delight of the crowd. 'We were there when Jensen scored' was sung for much of the remainder of the game, the crowd not seeming to care that QPR came back to win 3-1.

Jensen returned to Brondby in 1996, his goal against QPR being his only one in 132 appearances for Arsenal. In contrast, he scored four times in 69 matches for Denmark.

1995
DENNIS BERGKAMP ARRIVES FOR RECORD FEE

Arsenal tripled their transfer record in the summer of 1995 when they paid £7.5 million for Dutch international Dennis Bergkamp.

Bergkamp had made a name for himself at Ajax but had a frustrating two years with Inter Milan. This didn't deter Arsenal manager Bruce Rioch who smashed their previous transfer record, which stood at the £2.5 million paid for both Ian Wright and John Hartson.

The Dutchman was also reported to be the highest paid player in the British game but he started slowly, failing to score in his first six games. He finished the season with eleven league goals from 33 appearances, helping Arsenal qualify for the UEFA Cup.

After Arsene Wenger became manager in 1996 Bergkamp really thrived, his goals and assists helping the club to a third place finish. The following season, 1997-98, he was outstanding as Arsenal won the Double and he was voted both players' and writers' footballer of the year.

Bergkamp remained at Arsenal for eleven years, the latter part playing deeper and picking out the passes for players with younger legs. He retired at the end of 2005-06 aged 36, turning down a scouting role to spend more time with his family. He was voted number two in Arsenal.com's top fifty players and has a statue at the Emirates Stadium.

1996
FOUR MANAGERS
IN ONE YEAR

1996 was a revolving door for managers at Highbury, but the fourth arrival was the one that would prove to be a catalyst for the club's future success.

After George Graham was sacked, Arsenal appointed Bolton's Bruce Rioch and he guided the club to a fifth place finish in 1995-96. However he was sacked three weeks before the new season after a dispute over transfer funds.

Rioch's assistant Stewart Houston was appointed

caretaker manager and was in charge for the start of the season, but he resigned in the middle of September to take over at Queens Park Rangers.

By now it was widely reported that Arsenal's directors had identified former Monaco manager Arsene Wenger as Rioch's long term successor. However he was still contracted to Japanese club Grampus Eight and with negotiations still ongoing, former defender Pat Rice was appointed on an caretaker basis.

Rice was in charge for three games, all of which were won before Wenger finally took over on 1st October, keeping Rice on as his assistant. The reactions of many fans was 'Arsene Who' but twenty years later he was still at the club and has won more trophies than any other Arsenal manager

1996
THE ARRIVAL OF
PATRICK VIERA

When French midfielder Patrick Viera joined Arsenal early in the 1996-97 season it was an indication that the managerial situation at the club wasn't quite as it seemed.

In August 1996 the arrival of two Frenchmen, Remi Garde and Patrick Viera, led to press speculation that transfer dealings were being dictated by a manager yet to take over. Viera then gave the game away by telling the Daily Mirror that he was signing because Wenger could speak French.

Six feet four inches tall, Viera had a number of special attributes, being able to win the ball easily then distribute it with precision or keep hold of it and surge forward. He adapted to the English game with ease and his midfield partnership with Emmanuel Petit was instrumental in the Double triumph of 1997-98.

Viera was made captain in 2002 after Tony Adams retired and was captain for The Invincibles season of 2003-04. His last act in an Arsenal shirt was to score the decisive penalty in a shootout that won the FA Cup in 2005, before leaving for Juventus that summer. He had played 406 times for Arsenal, scoring 33 times.

1997
IAN WRIGHT BREAKS
CLIFF BASTIN'S RECORD

In 1997 Arsenal's goalscoring record was broken by a player whose signing wasn't universally welcomed.

Ian Wright cost a club record £2.5 million when he joined from Crystal Palace in 1991 aged 27. Many wondered if he was needed as Alan Smith had been the league's leading scorer twice in the previous three seasons.

Any reservations were dispelled immediately as Wright scored a hat-trick on his league debut at Southampton and finished 1991-92 as the league's leading scorer. He then scored in the following season's FA Cup final.

Dennis Bergkamp's arrival led to the pair forming an explosive partnership and as the goals kept coming he went into the 1997-98 season within touching distance of Cliff Bastin's fifty year old record.

On 13th September 1997 Arsenal faced Bolton at Highbury, with Wright scoring in the twentieth minute to equal Bastin's tally of 178 goals. Forgetting he needed another to break the record, he ripped off his shirt to display a t-shirt saying 179 - Just Done It. However five minutes later he scored a tap in and justifiably celebrated in style.

Wright left at the end of the season aged 34. His final tally of 185 was eventually beaten by Thierry Henry and he was ranked number four in an Arsenal.com poll of the club's top fifty players.

1998
A SECOND DOUBLE

In 1997-98 the decision to appoint Arsene Wenger as manager was vindicated as Arsenal won the league and FA Cup double for the second time.

The Gunners were unbeaten in their first twelve games although six of these were drawn. November and December were disappointing with four defeats in one six game period. At the turn of the year they were in sixth place, twelve points behind leaders Manchester United.

An unbeaten run in January and February lifted Arsenal up to second, then a 1-0 win over United at Old Trafford on 14th March took them within six points of the leaders but with three games in hand. The next seven games were all won, meaning victory in the final home game against Everton would secure the title. At an ecstatic Highbury Arsenal cruised to a 4-0 win, meaning it was irrelevant that the final two games, both away, were lost.

In the FA Cup the Gunners needed a penalty shoot out to beat Port Vale in the third round. They then beat Middlesbrough, Crystal Palace, West Ham and Wolverhampton to set up a final with Newcastle.

Goals from Marc Overmars and Nicolas Anelka were enough to win the cup for Arsenal, who emulated the achievement of Manchester United two years earlier by winning the Double for a second time.

1998
ARSENAL'S RECORD
80 HOME CROWD - AT WEMBLEY!

Arsenal's record attendance for a home game didn't come at Highbury or the Emirates but instead at Wembley, where they played Champions League games for two years.

With Highbury's 38,000 capacity needing to be further reduced to meet UEFA's media and advertising obligations, Arsenal opted to play their home games at Wembley to give as many fans as possible the chance to attend.

The Gunners qualified automatically for the group stages and were drawn alongside Dynamo Kiev, Lens and Panathinaikos. After drawing 1-1 in Lens in their opening game, 73,454 saw Arsenal beat Panathinaikos 2-1 in the first game at Wembley. In the next game at home to Dynamo Kiev the Gunners looked on course for victory only to concede a late equaliser.

After then losing 3-1 in Kiev Arsenal still had qualification in their own hands and the final home game against Lens was watched by a new club home record of 73,707. However the French side won 1-0 to eliminate the Gunners. The head to head rule for splitting sides who were level on points meant Arsenal had no chance of overhauling either Lends or Kiev.

Arsenal also played Champions League games at Wembley for the 1999-00 season, but the famous old stadium's demolition meant there was no option but to play at Highbury from 2000-01.

1999
THE REPLAYED
FA CUP MATCH

When Arsenal beat Sheffield United with a hotly disputed goal in the fifth round of the 1998-99 FA Cup, Arsene Wenger's offer to replay the game was accepted by the Football Association.

With the teams level at 1-1 Arsenal were rattled in the second half when Sheffield United hit the post. After the ball was kicked into touch for an opposition player to be treated, Arsenal's Kanu misread the situation when he intercepted a throw in back to the United keeper and squared the ball for Marc Overmars to score.

Kanu insisted he had not known about the injury and as it was an unwritten rule to give the ball back to the opposition in these circumstances, the goal had to stand. The score remained 2-1 and afterwards, Wenger offered to replay the game. This was accepted by United and the FA, who declared the result void.

Ten days later the sides met again with Arsenal winning by the same scoreline. This time though there was no controversy with them leading 2-0 through Overmars and Dennis Bergkamp, United scoring with a late consolation.

Arsenal went on to reach the semi-finals of the FA Cup where they were beaten by Manchester United after a replay.

2000
NO JOY ON
82 RETURN TO COPENHAGEN

Six years after winning the European Cup Winners Cup in Copenhagen, Arsenal were back there for the UEFA Cup final but failed to bring the trophy home.

Arsenal's European campaign began in the Champions League but after finishing third in their group they dropped into the UEFA Cup. The Gunners comfortably won two legged ties against Nantes, Deportivo La Coruna and Werder Bremen to reach the semi-finals, where they were drawn against Lens.

An early Dennis Bergkamp goal at Highbury gave the Gunners a narrow lead to take into the second leg. Shortly before half time in the Stade Felix Bollaert Thierry Henry scored a crucial away goal and although Lens equalised, Kanu scored late on to complete a 3-1 aggregate victory.

The opponents in the final were Galatasary, aiming to become the first Turkish club to win a European trophy. Both sides had plenty of chances but there were no goals after ninety minutes meaning extra time was necessary.

Despite having a player sent off Galatasary defended well to force a penalty shoot-out at the end where their supporters were gathered. Arsenal's Davor Šuker and Patrick Viera missed their kicks and Galatasary converted all of theirs to win 4-1. Afterwards Arsene Wenger said having the extra man wasn't necessarily an advantage as it helped the opposition focus even more.

2002
MILLENIUM MAGIC

After the disappointment of losing the 2001 FA Cup final, Arsenal made up for it the following year thanks to wonder goals from Ray Parlour and Fredrik Ljundberg.

With Wembley being rebuilt, cup finals were held at the Millennium Stadium in Cardiff between 2001 and 2006. In the first of these the Gunners dominated against Liverpool but conceded twice in the last seven minutes to lose 2-1, but there was to be no repeat a year later.

Arsenal had knocked Liverpool out in the fourth round and also eliminated fellow title challengers Newcastle. After beating Middlesbrough in the semi-final they faced Claudio Ranieri's Chelsea, winners of the last Wembley final two years earlier.

The game was fairly even until the 70th minute when Parlour collected a pass from Sylvain Wiltord on the left of the field and advanced to curl in a brilliant effort from 25 yards. Five minutes later Ljundberg sealed the victory with another great goal, shaking off the challenge of John Terry and firing home from the edge of the area.

After the game captain Tony Adams sportingly invited Patrick Viera, who had stood in for him for much of the season, to jointly lift the cup. The celebrations didn't go overboard though, as there was still a league title to secure.

2002
UNBEATEN AWAY
FROM HOME

When Arsenal won the league for the twelfth time in 2001-02 they did so without losing a single away game.

At the turn of the year Arsenal were top of the league but only on goal difference from Newcastle and Leeds, both of whom had won at Highbury. However the Gunners had remained unbeaten away from home, getting a crucial win at fellow title challengers Liverpool in the process.

On 2nd February Southampton held out for a 1-1 draw at Highbury, but this was to be the last time Arsenal dropped points all season. The following week they won 1-0 at Everton then beat Fulham 4-1 at home. On 2nd March they defeated Newcastle 2-0 at St James Park, but with ten games to go the top four teams were separated by just two points.

Arsenal continued winning and on 8th May they faced Manchester United at Old Trafford in their penultimate game. United were the only team who could overhaul the Gunners but Sylvain Wiltord's second half goal was enough to secure the title and complete the Double for the third time.

Three days later Everton were beaten 4-3 at Highbury meaning the season ended with just three defeats, all of them at home, as Charlton joined Newcastle and Leeds in winning at Highbury.

2003
WINNING THE
FA CUP INDOORS

When Arsenal won the FA Cup in 2002-03 they did so in the first final to be played indoors.

Bad weather meant the roof at the Millennium Stadium was closed for the final between the Gunners and Southampton, who had beaten Tottenham 4-0 back in the third round.

An injury to Patrick Viera meant keeper David Seaman was Arsenal's captain in what would be his last game for the club. The Gunners started off well, Thierry Henry having a shot saved in the first thirty seconds and Dennis Bergkamp having an eighth minute effort cleared off the line.

Seaman made a great save from Chris Baird but in the 38th minute Robert Pires gave Arsenal the lead, scoring after Fredrik Ljundberg's shot was saved.

In the second half the Gunners had chances to double their lead and on the whole withstood any Southampton pressure. There was an almighty scare in injury time however when James Beattie's goalbound header was cleared off the line by Ashley Cole.

Arsenal's victory made up for the disappointment of finishing ten points behind Manchester United in the league. It was the club's ninth FA Cup triumph and they became the first team since Tottenham in 1982 to retain the trophy.

2003
CESC FABREGAS,
86 ARSENAL'S YOUNGEST PLAYER

At the age of just 16 years and 177 days, Cesc Fabregas became Arsenal's youngest ever player in 2003-04.

A prolific scorer with Barcelona's youth teams, Fabregas joined Arsenal's academy on 11th September 2003. Less than two months later he was named in a youthful side that faced Rotherham in the League Cup at Highbury.

Fabregas did not look out of place in midfield and after a 1-1 draw the Gunners won 9-8 on penalties. In the following round he scored in a 5-1 win over Wolverhampton Wanderers but despite his promise he was unable to gain any league experience that season.

In 2004-05 he got more opportunities, becoming the club's youngest ever league player in the opening game of the season. As well as appearing in the Champions League he also started the FA Cup final.

The departure of Patrick Viera that summer was not a concern for Arsene Wenger with Fabregas at the club and he was handed the Frenchman's number four shirt, making forty appearances in 2005-06.

Nominated by his fellow professionals for the player of the year in both 2006-07 and 2007-08, Fabregas was appointed Arsenal's captain in 2008-09.

Fabregas returned to his boyhood club Barcelona in 2011 but three years later angered many Arsenal fans when he returned to London to join rivals Chelsea.

2004
THE INVINCIBLES

Arsenal's 2003-04 title triumph will go down in history due to going the whole season unbeaten.

The Gunners signalled their intent by winning their first four games. Sol Campbell and Kolo Toure were solid at the back, Patrick Viera and Robert Pires dominated the midfield and upfront Dennis Bergkamp and Thierry Henry were unstoppable.

Before Christmas there were big away wins; 4-0 at Middlesbrough, 4-1 at Leeds and 3-0 at Birmingham. At New Year the Gunners were still in second place but *The Times* described them as having 'an aura of invincibility'.

A nine match winning run opened up a nine point gap at the top, but hopes of a treble were dashed when Arsenal were knocked out of both the FA Cup and Champions League within a week. They then trailed Liverpool 2-1 at half time at Highbury, but came back after the break to win 4-2, Henry completing a hat-trick.

The title was secured with a 2-2 draw at Tottenham on 25th April. Arsenal didn't ease up in their final four games, drawing with Birmingham and Portsmouth then beating Fulham and Leicester to complete a remarkable season.

The final record was Played 38 Won 26 Drew 12 Lost 0. Not since Preston in 1888-89, a 22 game season, had a team gone a whole campaign unbeaten.

2004
A LEAGUE RECORD
UNBEATEN RUN

After 'The Invincibles' season Arsenal continued their unbeaten run into 2004-05 to break the record for the most league games without defeat.

Arsenal's last league defeat had been on 4th May 2003 when Leeds won 3-2 at Highbury. They finished that season with a 6-1 thrashing of Southampton at home then a 4-0 win at Sunderland.

The record unbeaten league run stood at 42 games, set by Nottingham Forest in 1977-78 and 1978-79, meaning Arsenal could break it if they avoided defeat in their first three games of 2004-05.

After a comfortable 4-1 win at Everton the Gunners opened their home campaign with a 5-3 win over Middlesbrough. Before that game they were presented with a golden replica of the Premier League trophy to commemorate the unbeaten season. The run extended to 43 games, a new record, with a 3-0 home win over Blackburn.

The Gunners then cruised to away wins at Norwich and Fulham before Bolton ended the 100% start by drawing 2-2 at Highbury. Wins over Manchester City, Charlton and Aston Villa followed, stretching the run to 49 games.

Finally, on 24th October 2004, The Invincibles were beaten. In a bad tempered game a Old Trafford, Manchester United won 2-0 with their first goal coming from a hotly disputed penalty.

2005
WINNING THE FA CUP
ON PENALTIES

When Arsenal won the FA Cup for the third time in four years, they became the first team to win the final on penalties.

The Gunners started off by beating Stoke and Wolverhampton at home before needing penalties to get past Sheffield United in the fifth round. After winning at Bolton in the sixth round, they eased to a 3-0 win over Blackburn in the semi-final.

Arsenal had finished second in the league, six points ahead of final opponents Manchester United but lost both meetings between the two clubs. United had also knocked them out of the League Cup.

With Thierry Henry injured Arsene Wenger opted to play with Denis Bergkamp as a lone striker and brought in Gilberto Silva as an extra midfielder.

The game was a dull affair played in the rain and Arsenal didn't have a shot on target until extra time. With seconds remaining Jose Reyes bodychecked Christiano Ronaldo and became only the second player to be sent off in an FA Cup final.

In the penalty shoot out Paul Scholes missed for United but all five of Arsenal's kicks were converted, the decisive one coming from Patrick Viera. After the match Wenger admitted Arsenal had been fortunate, but pointed to the loss against Liverpool in 2001 as proof that not always the best team wins.

2006
THE LAST MATCH
AT HIGHBURY

Arsenal moved out of their home of 93 years at the end of the 2005-06 season to take up residence at the Emirates Stadium.

To mark the last season at Highbury, Arsenal donned a maroon kit similar to the one that had been worn in 1913. There were some memorable moments on the pitch, including a 7-0 win over Middlesbrough and big European nights. Patrick Viera had left but Thierry Henry was magnificent, breaking Ian Wright's scoring record.

On Sunday 7th May 2006 the curtain came down on the famous old stadium with a home game against Wigan Athletic. Robert Pires scored for Arsenal but Wigan came back to lead 2-1. Henry then took control, equalising before half time and then scoring twice after the break, celebrating the penalty kick that completed his hat-trick by kneeling down and kissing the turf.

Dennis Bergkamp came off the bench for his final Highbury appearance and the celebrations were completed with the news that Spurs had lost at West Ham. Arsenal's 4-2 win meant they had pipped their great rivals to a Champions League place.

After the game there was a parade of legends before fans left for the last time. The Gunners then moved into the 60,000 capacity Emirates Stadium with Highbury being converted into an apartment complex.

MEANEST DEFENCE
IN THE CHAMPIONS LEAGUE

FACT 91

Arsenal set a competition record as they reached the final of the Champions League in 2005-06.

The Gunners began in the group stage with a 2-1 home win over Swiss side Thun, before beating Ajax by the same scoreline in Amsterdam. They then won three and drew one of the remaining matches without conceding a goal to top the group.

In the round of 16 Arsenal secured a famous win over Real Madrid, winning 1-0 in the Bernebeu Stadium then drawing 0-0 at the Emirates. In the quarter-final, a 2-0 home win over Juventus was followed up with a 0-0 draw in Turin.

Spanish side Villareal were the semi-final opponents and at the Emirates Kolo Toure gave the Gunners a slender lead. In the second leg Jens Lehmann saved a late penalty from Juan Riquelme, setting up a final with Barcelona in Paris.

After eighteen minutes Arsenal suffered a massive blow when Lehmann was sent off for bringing down Samuel Eto'o, but they still took the lead in the 37th minute through Sol Campbell. Arsenal held on until quarter of an hour from time when Eto'o equalised and Juliano Belletti got Barcelona's winner five minutes later.

The Gunners had lost the final although the 919 minutes they went without conceding a goal remains a Champions League record.

2007
THIERRY HENRY
LEAVES

In the summer of 2007 Thierry Henry, for many Arsenal's greatest ever player, left the club after eight years.

Arsene Wenger paid £11 million for Henry prior the 1999-00 season. Although he initially struggled, failing to score in his first eight games, he soon adapted to the English game and ended the season with 26 goals.

Henry was the club's leading scorer in 2000-01 and got 32 in all competitions as Arsenal won the Double in 2001-02. He passed the thirty goal mark in each of the next three seasons, winning the players and writers player of the year in 2003 and 2004.

2005-06 was a personal triumph for Henry, breaking both Ian Wright's overall scoring record and surpassing Cliff Bastin as the club's top league scorer. He was the Premier League's top scorer, was named in the FIFA XI and won the football writers player of the year award.

Unfortunately 2006-07 was marred by injuries and Henry played only seventeen league games, still managing ten goals. After the season ended he moved to Barcelona and the following summer he was voted number one in Arsenal.com's top fifty players.

In 2012 Henry, now aged 34 and with New York Red Bulls, returned to Arsenal on loan. He scored twice in seven appearances, bringing his final tally to 228 goals.

2008
MILANESE
DOUBLE

When Arsenal beat AC Milan in the Champions League round of sixteen in 2007-08 they became the first English team to beat both Milanese clubs in the San Siro stadium that they share.

In November 2003 Arsenal travelled to the San Siro to face Inter Milan in the penultimate game of the group stage. Thierry Henry gave Arsenal the lead midway through the first half but Christian Vieri equalised before half time. In a stunning second half goals from Fredrik Ljundberg, Henry, Edu and Robert Pires gave the Gunners a stunning 5-1 win.

In the draw for the first knockout round in 2007-08 Arsenal were drawn against AC Milan. After a 0-0 draw at the Emirates the Gunners took the game to Milan in the second leg. They dominated the game and it was no surprise when Cesc Fabregas finally broke the deadlock six minutes from time with a thirty yard drive. Adebayor added a second in injury time and there was sporting applause from the home side at the end of the game.

Arsenal had achieved something that no English club has done before or since. There would be no such luck in their next visit to the San Siro though in 2011-12 when they lost 4-0 to AC Milan.

2009
TWENTY GAMES UNBEATEN
AGAINST TOTTENHAM

Arsenal's 3-0 home win over Spurs on 31st October 2009 stretched the Gunners' unbeaten league run against their rivals to twenty games.

The run started on 19th March 2000 when Arsenal won 2-1 in the North London derby at Highbury. Eleven of the twenty games were won and nine drawn.

Of the eleven games in which Arsenal were the home side, the Gunners won nine of them. This should really have been ten but in 2008-09 Spurs scored twice in the closing stages, coming from 4-2 down to draw 4-4.

Away from home Arsenal won twice, including an incredible 5-4 win in 2004-05 in which Spurs had scored the opening goal before the Gunners hit back to lead 3-1, 4-2 and 5-3.

Arsenal's leading scorer during the unbeaten run was Robert Pires with seven, while Emmanuel Adebayor got six and Thierry Henry five.

The run finally came to an end on 14th April 2010 when Arsenal lost 2-1 at White Hart Lane. This was Spurs first league win in the fixture since the Millennium and the following season they won at the Emirates for the first time, coming from 2-0 down to win 3-2.

2010
A NEW
ARSENAL CLOCK

In the first home fixture of 2010-11 there was a return to the past as a new Arsenal Clock was installed and two stands renamed.

Previously the stands at the Emirates had simply been north, south, east and west. However after consultation with supporters, it was agreed to rename the North Stand the North Bank and the South Stand the Clock End, in honour of the previous ends at Highbury.

The famous clock at Highbury was initially situated on the North Bank and was a 45 minute clock, allowing fans to see how long was left of the half. The FA weren't happy though as it could undermine officials and it was changed to a normal clock and moved to the South Terrace in 1935, which then became the Clock End.

The original clock is now situated outside of the stadium, while a replica measuring 2.6 metres in diameter was in place for the start of 2010-11. Fans could see it at the pre-season Emirates Cup but it was officially welcomed at the first home league game with Blackpool, when huge banners also celebrated the renaming of the North Bank and Clock End.

2011
STATUES OF
THREE LEGENDS

As part of Arsenal's 125th anniversary, three statues of club legends were unveiled outside the Emirates Stadium on 9th December 2011.

The bronze statues were of legendary manager Herbert Chapman, the club's most successful captain Tony Adams and record goalscorer Thierry Henry. They are one and a half times the size of the men in real life and weigh 200 kilograms each.

Chapman's statue has him stood with his hands behind his back looking towards the stadium. Adams is depicted with his arms outstretched, the way he celebrated his goal in the 4-0 win over Everton in 1998 that confirmed Arsenal as champions. Henry's statue has been cast in the pose he took after scoring a wonder goal against Tottenham in November 2002.

Unveiling the statues, chairman Peter Hill-Wood said 'Today is a celebration of three hugely influential figures in the history of Arsenal Football Club. These legends are now proudly on display outside Emirates Stadium for all to see'.

In 2014 further statues were unveiled of former player Dennis Bergkamp and Ken Friar, who since 1945 has served the club in a variety of roles, from matchday messenger to secretary and managing director.

2013
CLUB TRANSFER
RECORD SMASHED

With just hours to go on transfer deadline day in 2013, Arsenal smashed their club transfer record to bring German international Mesut Özil to the Emirates Stadium.

The signing of the attacking midfielder was completed at 10.30pm on 2nd September, a few hours after the Spanish giants had paid a world record £86 million for Tottenham's Gareth Bale. Özil had a medical in Germany where he was with his national squad preparing for a World Cup qualifier.

The fee was £42.5 million, nearly triple the £15 million which had been spent on Andrey Arshavin in 2009. It signalled a clear statement of intent from Arsenal, the transfer being at the time was the third most expensive in English football history.

Özil was described in the *Guardian* newspaper as the 'king of the assist' and on his debut took just eleven minutes to set up a goal for Olivier Giroud away to Sunderland.

In his first two seasons Özil got more assists than anyone else in the Premiership, a feat made more impressive as he had a three month spell on the sidelines with a knee injury, In 2015-16 his total of twenty assists and eight goals in all competitions led to him being named player of the season by fans.

2014
COME BACK FROM 2-0
DOWN TO WIN CUP

When Arsenal won their first trophy in nine years in 2013-14 they did it the hard way, coming from 2-0 down to beat Hull City in the FA Cup final.

The Gunners were drawn at home in every round, beating Tottenham, Coventry, Liverpool and Everton. There was a scare in the semi-final against Championship side Wigan, who took the lead before Per Mertesacker equalised eight minutes from time. In the penalty shoot-out Arsenal won 4-2, Lukasz Fabianski saving two spot kicks.

Arsenal got off to the worst possible start in the final against Hull City, conceding twice in the first eight minutes. Alex Bruce almost made it 3-0 but his header was cleared off the line from Kieran Gibbs. In the sixteenth minute Santi Corzola scored from a free kick and the score remained 2-1 at half time.

Laurent Koscielny got Arsenal's equaliser in the 71st minute and Olivier Giroud almost scored an injury time winner but his shot was saved. He then hit the bar early in extra time before setting up Aaron Ramsey for the winning goal in the second period.

Arsenal's held on to win their first trophy since winning the FA Cup in 2005. It was their eleventh triumph in the competition, equalling Manchester United's record.

RECORDS BROKEN
AS CUP RETAINED

Arsenal broke records as they won the FA Cup in 2014-15, with the final also being much more straightforward than the previous season.

The Gunners defeated Hull, Brighton, Middlesbrough and Manchester United in the early rounds. For the second year running they faced a Championship side in the semi-final, beating Reading 2-1 after extra time to reach a record nineteenth final.

Their opponents were Aston Villa, who had beaten

Liverpool in the other semi-final. The Gunners were dominant from the start and the only surprise was that it took forty minutes for them to take the lead through Theo Walcott.

Early in the second half Alexis Sanchez scored a stunning goal from thirty yards and after that Villa capitulated. Per Mertesacker headed a third just after the hour and there could well have been many more goals. In the end there was just one, from Olivier Giroud in injury time, completing a miserable afternoon for Villa who didn't even have a shot on target.

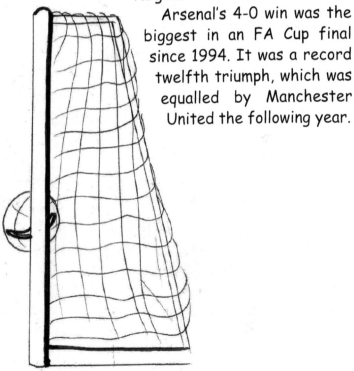

Arsenal's 4-0 win was the biggest in an FA Cup final since 1994. It was a record twelfth triumph, which was equalled by Manchester United the following year.

FACT 100
19 SUCCESSIVE CHAMPIONS LEAGUE CAMPAIGNS

In 2015-16 Arsenal's second placed finish ensured Champions League participation for the nineteenth season running the following season, a record bettered only by Real Madrid.

Home games for the Gunners' first two Champions League campaigns were played at Wembley and both times they failed to get out of their group. In 2000-01 with Highbury as a home venue they got through two sets of group stages before losing the quarter-final against Valencia.

2001-02 saw Arsenal eliminated in the second group stage and the following season they failed to get out of their group. In 2003-04 they made it to the quarter-finals, losing to London rivals Chelsea.

After losing in the round of sixteen in 2004-05 Arsenal made it to the final in 2005-06, where they lost to Barcelona. The following season they lost in the round of sixteen then in 2007-08 were eliminated by Liverpool in the quarter-final.

In 2008-09 the Gunners got to the semi-final but were beaten by Manchester United and they were knocked out by Barcelona in each of the next two seasons, first in the quarter-final then the round of sixteen.

The defeat to Barcelona in 2010-11 was the start of six successive defeats at the round of sixteen stage. Arsenal have also fallen to AC Milan, Bayern Munich (two seasons running), Monaco and Barcelona.

The 100 Facts Series

Arsenal, *Steve Horton*	978-1-908724-09-0
Aston Villa, *Steve Horton*	978-1-908724-92-2
Celtic, *Steve Horton*	978-1-908724-10-6
Chelsea, *Kristian Downer*	978-1-908724-11-3
Leeds, *Steve Horton*	978-1-908724-79-3
Liverpool, *Steve Horton*	978-1-908724-13-7
Manchester City, *Steve Horton*	978-1-908724-14-4
Manchester United, *Iain McCartney*	978-1-908724-15-1
Newcastle United, *Steve Horton*	978-1-908724-16-8
Norwich City, *Steve Horton*	978-1-908724-93-9
Rangers, *David Clayton*	978-1-908724-17-5
Tottenham Hostpur, *Steve Horton*	978-1-908724-18-2
West Ham, *Steve Horton*	978-1-908724-80-9

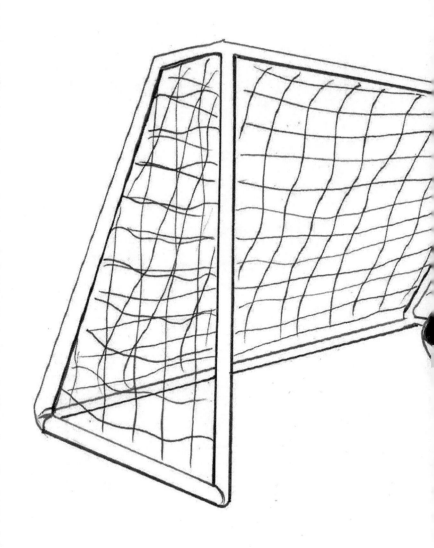